POP CULTURE REVOLUTIONS

GRAPHIC CONTENT!

The Culture of Comic Books

by Natalie M. Rosinsky

Content Adviser: Marc Tyler Nobleman, Cartoonist and Author of *Boys of Steel: The Creators of Superman*

Reading Adviser: Alexa L. Sandmann, Ed.D., Professor of Literacy, College and Graduate School of Education, Health, and Human Services, Kent State University

COMPASS POINT BOOKS
a capstone imprint

Compass Point Books
151 Good Counsel Drive
Box 669
Mankato, MN 56002-0669

Printed in the United States of America in North Mankato, Minnesota.
092009
005618CGS10

This book was manufactured with paper containing at least 10 percent post-consumer waste.

Managing Editor: Catherine Neitge
Designer: Veronica Bianchini
Photo Researcher: Eric Gohl
Library Consultant: Kathleen Baxter
Production Specialist: Jane Klenk

Library of Congress Cataloging-in-Publication Data
Rosinsky, Natalie M. (Natalie Myra)
Graphic content! : the culture of comic books / by Natalie M. Rosinsky.
p. cm.—(Pop culture revolutions)
Includes bibliographical references and index.
ISBN 978-0-7565-4241-2 (library binding)
1. Comic books, strips, etc.—United States—History and criticism—Juvenile literature. I. Title. II. Series.
PN6725.R67 2010
741.5'97309—dc22 2009030751

Visit Compass Point Books on the Internet at *www.compasspointbooks.com*
or e-mail your request to *custserv@compasspointbooks.com*

Image Credits ©: AP Images: 22, 31, Al Behrman, 52, Ann Johansson, 47, Anthony Camerano, 33, Charles Kenneth, cover, 28, Lenny Ignelzi, 24; BONE ® is © 2010 Jeff Smith, 16; Capstone Press, background; Corbis: EPA/Alberto Estevez, 45, Reuters/Daniel Aguilar, 37; Courtesy of Army Art Collection, U.S. Army Center of Military History, 26; Getty Images: AFP/William West, 56–57, AFP/Yoshikazu Tsuno, 5, 51, CBS Photo Archive, 43, 46, Chad Buchanan, 54–55, Hulton Archive, 17, 36, Mario Tama, 40, Time Life Pictures/Alfred Eisenstaedt, 11, Time Life Pictures/Carl Iwasaki, 34–35, WireImage/Gregg DeGuire, 53; The Granger Collection, New York: 4, ullstein bild, 6; Library of Congress, 8, 15, 23, 27, 29, 32; National Archives and Records Administration, 30; Newscom: 18, 44, ANP photo by Ton Koene, 10, 48–49, KRT Kids Elements, 14–15, SHNS photo courtesy Captain Comics/*The Commercial Appeal*, 25, SHNS photo courtesy Cartoon Network, 39, SHNS photo courtesy DC Comics, 38, SHNS photo courtesy Marvel Comics, 20, 21, 42, SHNS photo courtesy *The Commercial Appeal*, 13, WENN, 7, 59; Public domain, 9; Shutterstock/Binkski, 63.

TABLE OF CONTENTS

From Pulp Fiction to Prizewinners

Donald Duck in Sweden? Teenage superheroes with problems just like yours? People imprisoned or executed for creating comic books? The life of Buddha honored in a graphic novel? Get ready to be astonished by the pop culture blaze sparked and kept alive today by comic books.

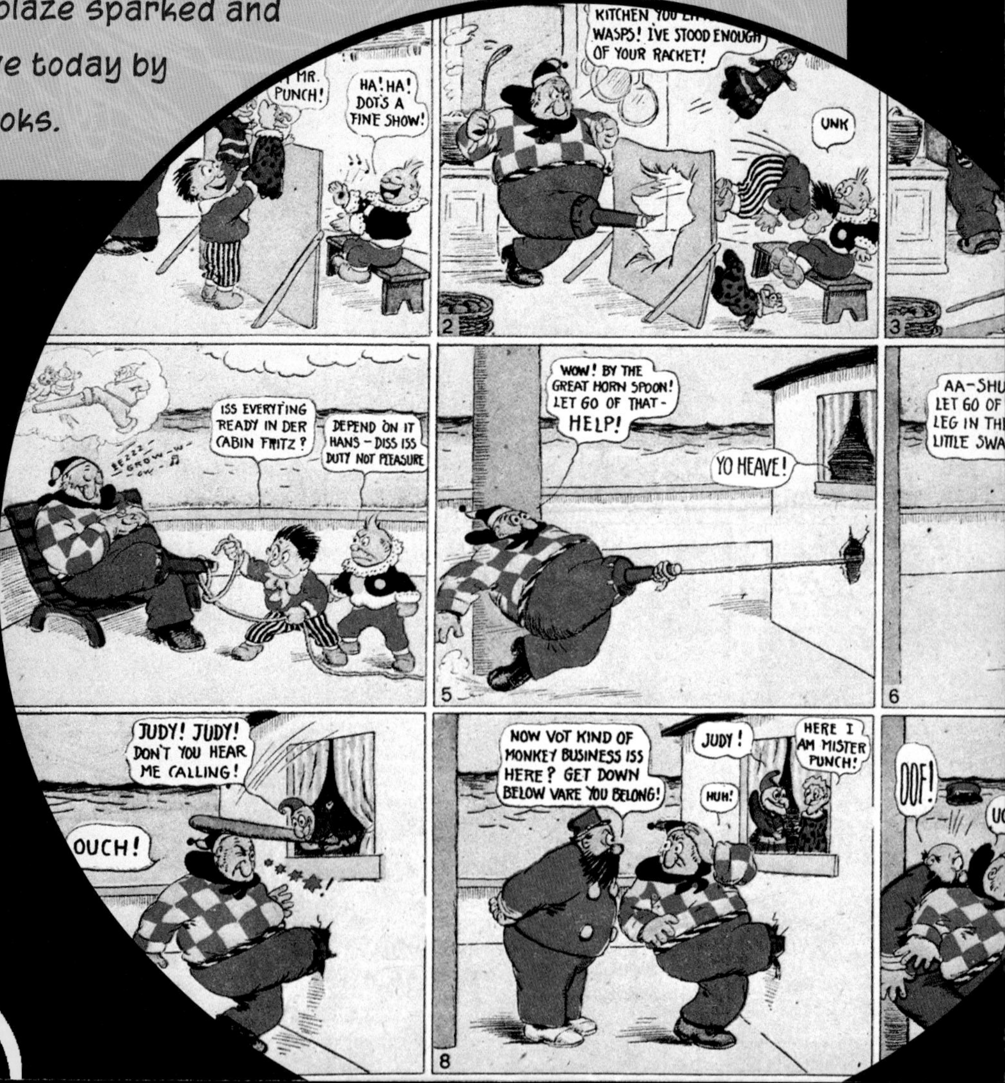
MR. PUNCH!
HA! HA! DOT'S A FINE SHOW!
WASPS! I'VE STOOD ENOUGH OF YOUR RACKET!
UNK
ISS EVERYTING READY IN DER CABIN FRITZ?
DEPEND ON IT HANS - DISS ISS DUTY NOT PLEASURE
WOW! BY THE GREAT HORN SPOON! LET GO OF THAT - HELP!
YO HEAVE!
JUDY! JUDY! DON'T YOU HEAR ME CALLING!
OUCH!
NOW VOT KIND OF MONKEY BUSINESS ISS HERE? GET DOWN BELOW VARE YOU BELONG!
JUDY!
HUH!
HERE I AM MISTER PUNCH!
OOF!

From short strips printed on cheap paper to award-winning novels—comic books have come a long way. Their evolution mirrors the way our world has become more complicated and connected in the last 100 years. The great news? These exciting changes are not over yet.

The first comic books charmed readers with humor, fantasy, and mysterious adventures. Later these popular works continued to win readers by championing or challenging beliefs. In times of war and social change, comic books told tales shaped by those sometimes troubling events and concerns. Comic books themselves became a source of controversy. Were they influencing people for good or bad? Some governments passed laws to censor comics. Other governments also feared the challenges presented by some comic books. Their officials approved horrible acts against comic book creators.

For many years, the U.S. comic book industry influenced readers and comic book creators in other countries. Since the 1980s, though, new technologies and other advances have shifted this balance. Foreign comic book cultures now have a large impact on U.S. readers and others around the globe. You might say that the worldwide web of comics is even bigger and stronger than Spider-Man's! Comic book stories and characters now find audiences through TV, movies, video games, and other technologies as well as the printed page.

A comic book by any other name

Comic books are called:

- *historietas*—"little stories" in Mexico
- *manga*—"irresponsible pictures" in Japan
- *gekiga*—"dramatic pictures" in Japan, by fans who prefer this more positive name
- *manhua*—"comics" in China
- *manhwa*—"comics" in South Korea
- *bande dessinée* (BD)—"drawn strip" in France
- *fumetti*—"speech bubbles" in Italy

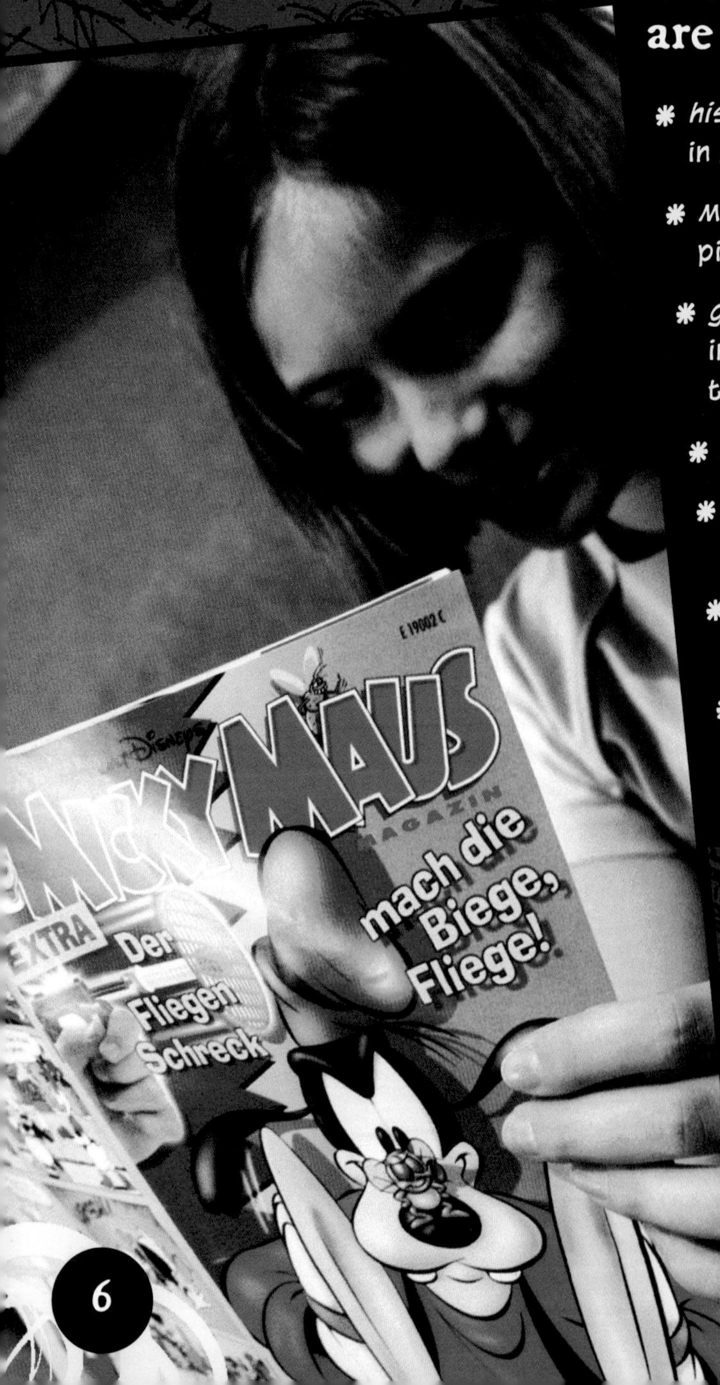
E 19002 C
MAUS
MAGAZIN
mach die Biege, Fliege!
EXTRA
Der Fliegen Schreck

Comic books have moved far from their humble beginnings. They have come off the street corner and out of the shadows. Awards ceremonies spotlight comic book achievements, and museums chronicle their history. Graphic novels—book-length comics—now compete with text-only books and win awards for achievement in literature. And—true to their history—some comic book creators continue to use their art to question society and promote social change. This pop culture revolution is still happening! Curious? Just turn the page …

Tintin, boy reporter

Since 1929 the adventures of European newspaper reporter Tintin have been published in more than 50 languages around the world. His French-speaking creator Hergé (born Georges Remi in Belgium) was a Boy Scout. He gave young Tintin many positive Scout traits. The well-educated young reporter roamed the globe and even traveled to the Moon.

Tintin appeared in newspaper strips before being featured in a magazine and in comic books that collected these strips. More than 230 million copies of Tintin comic books have been sold. Award-winning movie directors Steven Spielberg and Peter Jackson teamed to work on a series of three animated Tintin films.

CHAPTER 1

Charming Kids and Creatures

In the United States, newspaper comic strips appeared years before the first comic books. Some of the strips' most popular characters were mischief-making kids.

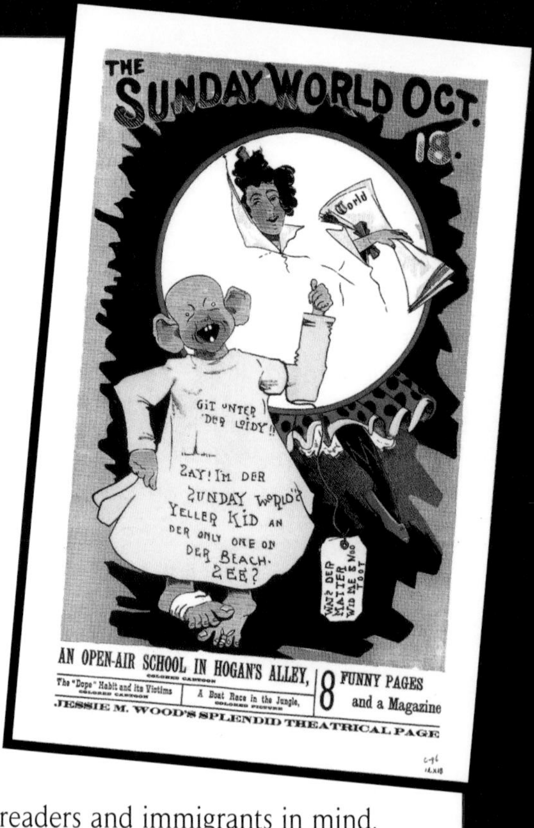

THE SUNDAY WORLD OCT. 18.
World
GIT UNTER DER LAIDY!!
SAY! I'M DER SUNDAY WORLD'S YELLER KID AN DER ONLY ONE ON DER BEACH. SEE?
AN OPEN-AIR SCHOOL IN HOGAN'S ALLEY, COLORED CARTOON
The "Dope" Habit and its Victims COLORED CARTOON
A Boat Race in the Jungle, COLORED PICTURE
8 FUNNY PAGES and a Magazine
JESSIE M. WOOD'S SPLENDID THEATRICAL PAGE

The Yellow Kid, created by Richard F. Outcault in the 1890s, lived in the crowded slums of New York City. His shaved head was typical of poor kids there, many of whom had head lice. The Yellow Kid—who got his name from his big yellow shirt—spoke slang. He used "de" for "the" and "dem" instead of "them." The Yellow Kid's adventures in *Hogan's Alley* and elsewhere appealed to readers of all backgrounds. Yet his pluck and determination were particularly popular with working-class readers. Like the original German-accented *Katzenjammer Kids,* created by Rudolph Dirks for a rival newspaper, stories about comic strip rascals were written with less-educated readers and immigrants in mind. These readers, many of whom were not fluent in English, could more easily read the comics because of the pictures.

Talking animals such as silly Krazy Cat, Ignatz Mouse, and Officer Pup were also popular comic strip characters. The funny pages increased the sales of newspapers. Toys associated with the characters also sold well.

A Funny Story

Readers loved the large sections of comics that were printed in several newspapers. So publishers had a ready-made market of readers eager to buy books of collected comic strips. By 1933, when the Dell Company published *Famous Funnies: A Carnival of Comics,* people were willing to pay a whole 10 cents (worth about $1.65 today) to buy this brand-new product—a comic book. The first comic book containing all-new material, *New Fun #1,* came along two years later.

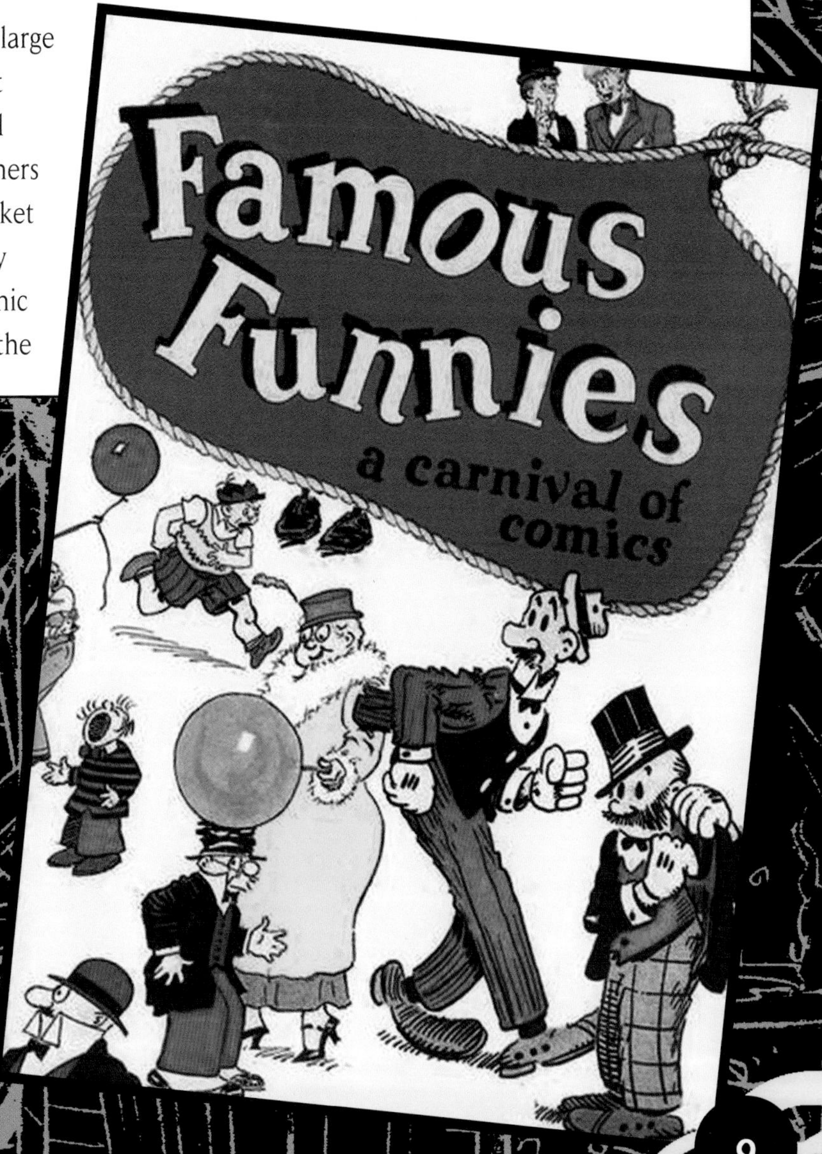
Famous Funnies
a carnival of comics

Comic books have come in all sizes.

The first free comic book newspaper inserts were big—half the size of a daily newspaper page.

By 1933 most U.S. comic books were smaller—the size of a business letter.

Today most U.S. comic books are slightly smaller than a business letter.

In Japan weekly or monthly serialized manga are still newspaper size.

In Japan and the rest of the world, reprinted collections of popular manga are much smaller—the size of a paperback book.

Today U.S. comics are typically 32 pages long, but Japanese manga can be 300 pages long.

In 2009 DC Comics honored comic book history with a blast from the past. It issued 12 comics that were the size of daily newspapers. These Wednesday Comics were inserts in the newspaper USA Today and were sold separately in stores.

The cartoon crowd

In the 1930s and 1940s, cartoons shown in movie theaters provided comic book publishers with more funny creatures and kids. Moviegoers loved Walt Disney's cartoon characters. Mickey Mouse, Donald Duck, and their friends and relatives made *Walt Disney's Comics and Stories* a best-selling series for more than 40 years. These characters remain popular today—as anyone who has ever visited or dreamed of visiting Disneyland knows.

Other movie companies also sold the rights to their cartoon characters to comic book publishers. Bugs Bunny, Porky Pig, and Woody Woodpecker all appeared in animated cartoons before they were featured in comic books. Casper the Friendly Ghost and Little Audrey also moved from the big screen to the printed page.

In the 1950s and 1960s, TV cartoons such as *The Rocky and Bullwinkle Show* inspired comic books.

Walt Disney's characters star in cartoons, movies, and comics.

Daffy about Donald Duck

Donald Duck, a Disney cartoon character enjoyed around the world, is more popular in Scandinavia than in the United States! Since 1948 generations of Swedes, Finns, Norwegians, and Danes have read comic books featuring Donald and his wacky family. In Sweden today, more than 400,000 people read each issue of a comic titled *Kalle Anka & Co (Donald Duck & Company)*. In Finland people buy 270,000 copies of every Donald Duck comic published there. In contrast, a typical comic book in the U.S. sells about 20,000 copies. The Finnish post office in 2001 even issued a special Donald Duck stamp. It celebrated the 50th anniversary of Finland's first published Donald Duck comic book. One of four Norwegians reads a Donald Duck comic each week. That is more than a million readers.

This popularity even led to a legal battle. In 1989 the Walt Disney Company sued the Swedish publisher of a comic book titled *Arne Anka (Arnie the Duck)*. Disney claimed that Arne—who smoked, swore, and got drunk—looked too much like wholesome Donald. Disney won its case, and the publisher changed Arne's appearance.

What is a comic book worth?

In 1962 the price of a new comic in the United States rose to 12 cents.

In 1969 the price rose again to 15 cents.

By 1991 a comic book cost $1.

In 2009 the price of regular monthly

Crazy cats

Today sly and greedy Garfield the Cat and Get Fuzzy's Satchel Pooch and Bucky Katt continue the comic strip tradition begun with *Krazy Cat* nearly 100 years ago.

Donald Duck, the enemy?

Has the popularity of Donald Duck comics in Latin America harmed people there? Well-known Chilean-American writer Ariel Dorfman thinks so. He says these books send destructive messages about unpaid labor and natural resources. When Uncle Scrooge ordered his nephews on dangerous treasure hunts, he never paid them. Huey, Dewey, and Louie traded small amounts of money for treasures found on their trips, or just took them, since their owners usually did not understand their value. Dorfman says these tales made people believe it was fair to pay Latin American workers very little. He also says these comic books suggested that foreign companies had the right to mine and harvest Latin American resources. What do you think about Dorfman's ideas?

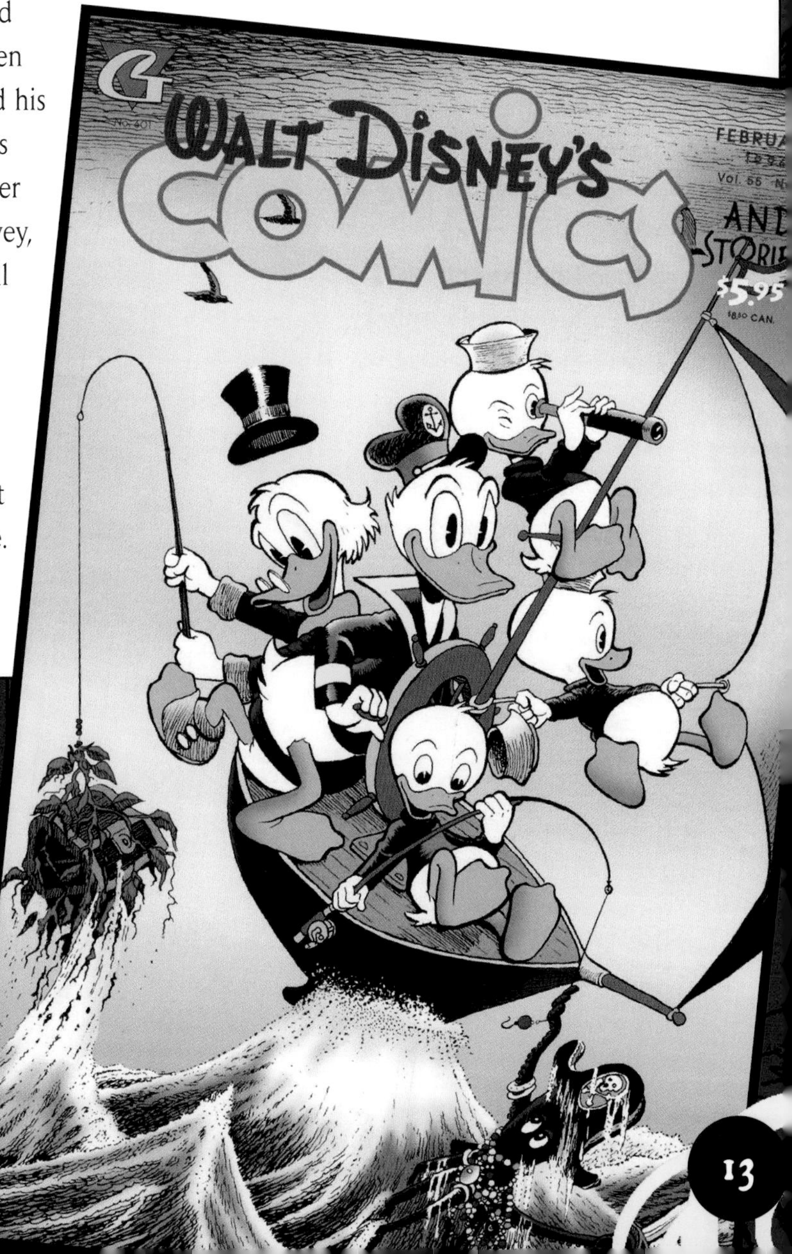
WALT DISNEY'S
COMICS
$5.95

Astro Boy, robot with heart

Since 1951 Tetsuwan Atom (Astro Boy) has become one of the best known characters in Japanese manga. Readers are touched by the adventures of this robot, designed by a grieving scientist to look like his son, who has died. The tales raise questions about what being human really means.

Osamu Tezuka, the creator of Astro Boy, is considered the father of Japanese manga. He was influenced by U.S. movies and Disney cartoons he saw when he was young. In 1963 Tezuka combined his interests in comics and cartoons to produce an animated  series featuring Astro Boy. Nearly 200 episodes of this anime series have been seen around the world. A movie-length anime of Astro Boy was released in 2009.

That's not just *Peanuts!*

Charles Schulz' *Peanuts* comic strips first appeared in U.S. newspapers in 1950. Since then, the adventures of Charlie Brown, Lucy, blanket-clutching Linus, Peppermint Patty, Snoopy, and Woodstock have become known around the world. They have been featured in comic books and paperback book collections. Readers enjoy the longer, self-contained stories that comic books—unlike strips—provide. TV specials and animated movies also feature this popular gang. Since it first aired in 1965, the TV special *A Charlie Brown Christmas* has become a yearly tradition. It is shown at least twice each December. *You're A Good Man, Charlie Brown* is a frequently produced musical play.

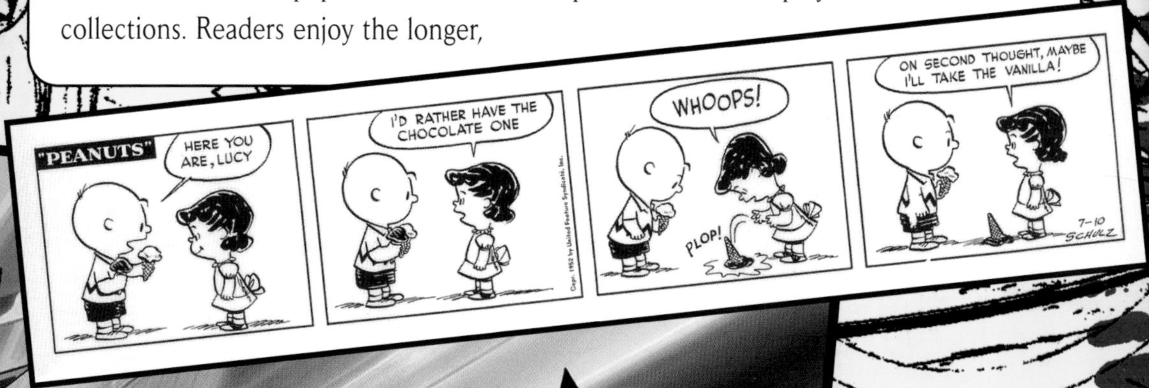
"PEANUTS"
HERE YOU ARE, LUCY
I'D RATHER HAVE THE CHOCOLATE ONE
Copr. 1952 by United Feature Syndicate, Inc.
WHOOPS!
PLOP!
ON SECOND THOUGHT, MAYBE I'LL TAKE THE VANILLA!
7-10
SCHULZ

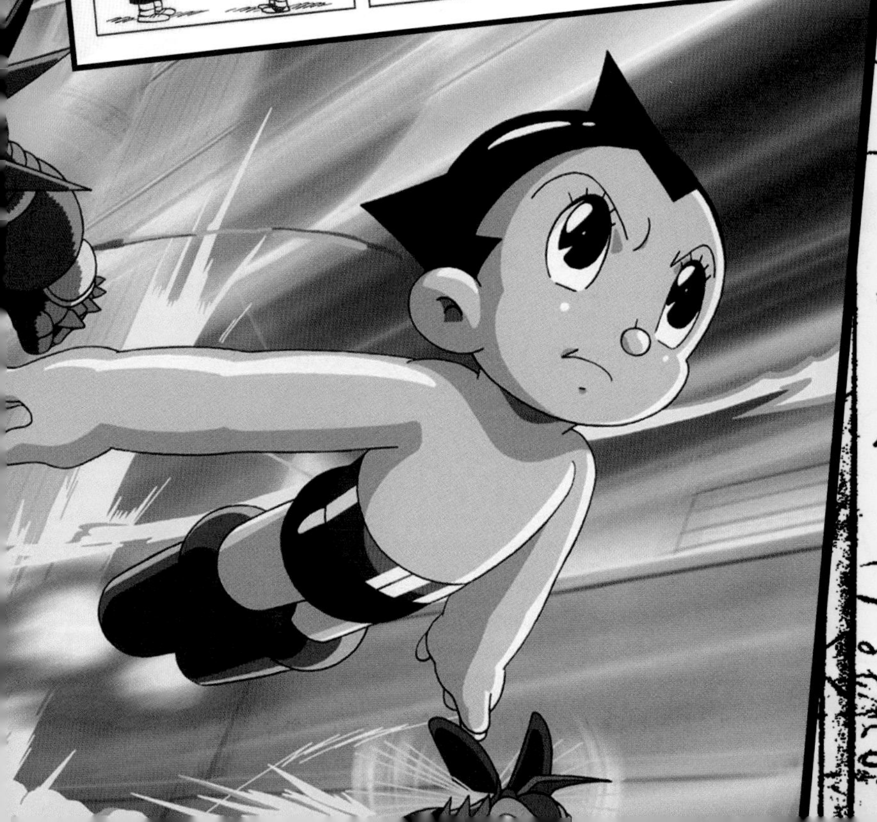

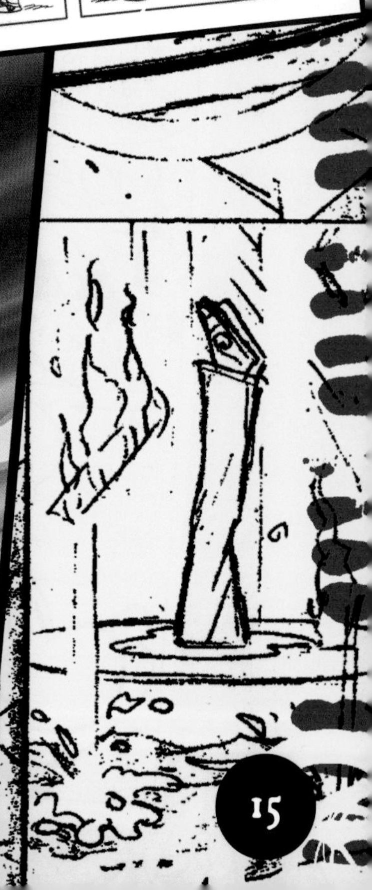

What *are* those creatures?

Some popular comic book creatures lefy description. The Moomins—first 'esigned by Finnish creator Tove Jansson ı the 1940s—are white, round, and ırry. Although Moomins are supposed be trolls, each one looks a bit like a ppopotamus.

The Marsupilami, created by Belgian :ist Andre Franquin in the 1950s, black-spotted, yellow-skinned, nkeylike creatures. They can breathe underwater and use their 7-foot-long (2-meter) tails to punch or push away attackers. Like the popular Moomins, the incredible Marsupilami have also been featured in TV shows.

U.S. comic book creator Jeff Smith's Bone Family are among these hard-to-identify characters. Fone Bone, Smiley Bone, and Phoney Bone are smaller than humans, totally white and bald, and big-nosed. Yet they have all the emotions, virtues, and vices of the "regular" people who inhabit Smith's fantasy world.

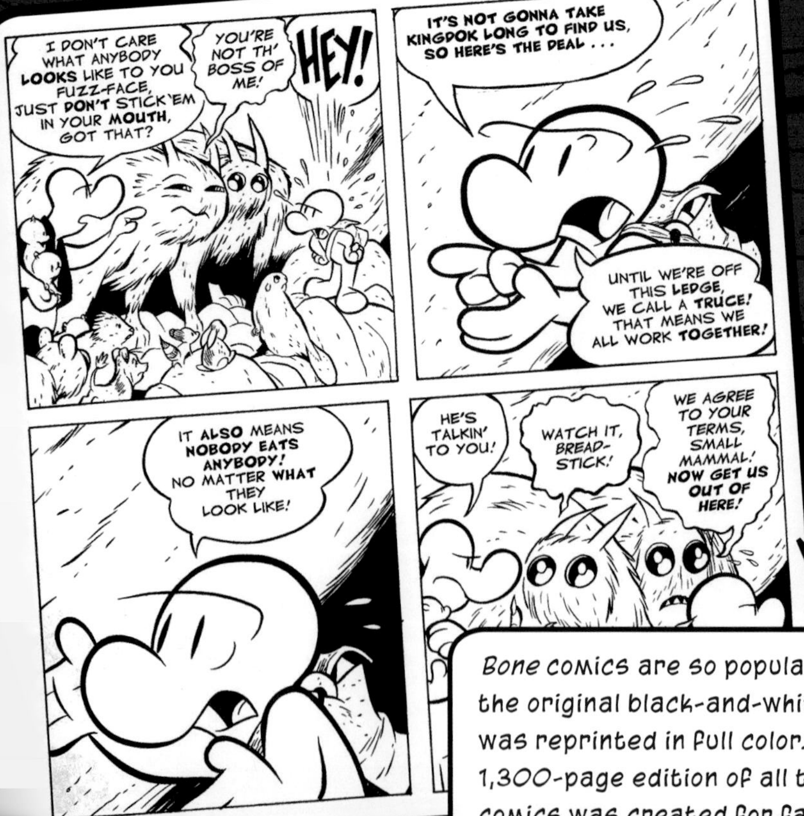
I DON'T CARE WHAT ANYBODY LOOKS LIKE TO YOU FUZZ-FACE, JUST DON'T STICK 'EM IN YOUR MOUTH, GOT THAT?
YOU'RE NOT TH' BOSS OF ME!
HEY!
IT'S NOT GONNA TAKE KINGDOK LONG TO FIND US, SO HERE'S THE DEAL . . .
UNTIL WE'RE OFF THIS LEDGE, WE CALL A TRUCE! THAT MEANS WE ALL WORK TOGETHER!
IT ALSO MEANS NOBODY EATS ANYBODY! NO MATTER WHAT THEY LOOK LIKE!
HE'S TALKIN' TO YOU!
WATCH IT, BREAD-STICK!
WE AGREE TO YOUR TERMS, SMALL MAMMAL! NOW GET US OUT OF HERE!

Bone comics are so popular that the original black-and-white series was reprinted in full color. A special 1,300-page edition of all the *Bone* comics was created for fans.

Facing the
Challenges of War

Even before World War II began, some comic book creators thought about the need to fight for freedom.

Writer Jerry Siegel said he created the character of Superman after "hearing and reading of the oppression and slaughter of helpless, oppressed Jews in Nazi Germany. ... How could I help them ... ? Superman was the answer." Drawn by artist Joe Shuster, the first Superman adventure appeared in *Action Comics #1*, dated June 1938.

JUNE, 1938

No. 1

ACTION COMICS

10¢

Batman joined the ranks of crime fighters a year later, in *Detective Comics #27* (May 1939).

Unlike Superman—whose birth on another planet gave him extraordinary powers—Batman was a human being who depended on special equipment and training to defeat evildoers. Batman's battle against crime in Gotham City was an extreme version of already popular plots. Crime-fighting detectives, police officers, adventurers, and cowboys were regular characters in some 1930s pulp magazines and comics. But after war broke out in September 1939, battling crime on the home front became less important in comics than defeating the enemy. Comic book creators soon produced a horde of superheroes whose war efforts inspired readers.

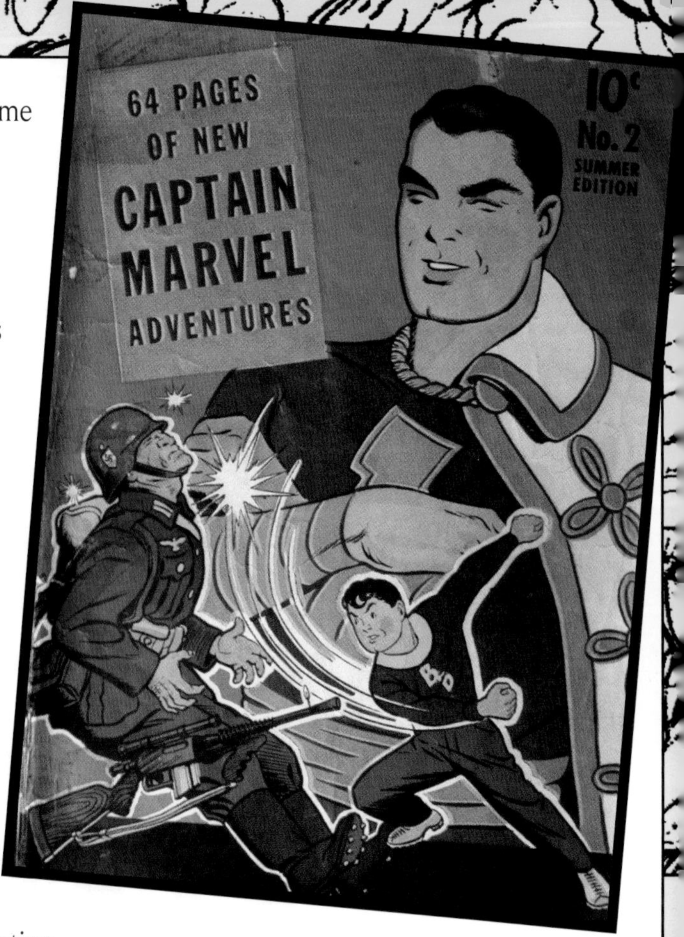
64 PAGES OF NEW
CAPTAIN MARVEL ADVENTURES
10¢
No. 2
SUMMER EDITION

SHAZAM!

The Flash, Green Lantern, Wonder Woman, and Captain Marvel all fought wartime enemies as well as ordinary criminals. One reason Captain Marvel was a special favorite of young readers is that he was an adult superhero whose secret identity was a boy—radio announcer Billy Batson. By saying the magic word "SHAZAM!," Billy instantly became "the world's mightiest mortal." Can you imagine how many kids tried *that* at home?

After the United States entered the war in December 1941, superheroes Captain Marvel Jr. (Freddy Freeman) and 14-year-old Mary Marvel (Mary Batson) joined her brother Billy in the war effort. Like Wonder Woman, Mary Marvel and other female characters such as Miss America and Liberty Belle fought spies and other enemies, but not on the front lines. In the 1940s, it was not considered proper for women, even super powerful ones, to serve in combat.

SHAZAM, a powerful WORD

When Billy Batson said "SHAZAM!" he was calling up the powers of these ancient heroes and supposed gods:

WISDOM OF SOLOMON

STRENGTH OF HERCULES

STAMINA OF ATLAS

POWER OF ZEUS

COURAGE OF ACHILLES

SPEED OF MERCURY

When Mary Batson used the magic word, she conjured up these powers:

GRACE OF SELENA

STRENGTH OF HIPPOLYTA

SKILL OF ARIADNE

FLEETNESS OF ZEPHYRUS

BEAUTY OF AURORA

WISDOM OF MINERVA

Captain America

The cover of the first *Captain America* comic book in 1941 showed the title character knocking out Adolf Hitler, the dictator of Nazi Germany. This punch was especially significant to readers because Captain America—like Batman—did not have super powers. In his everyday life, Steve Rogers was an ordinary, even sickly man. Yet when he was given a secret, experimental government serum, Rogers, as Captain America, achieved the peak of human abilities. People who believed the United States should enter World War II were thrilled by this superhero's deeds. Others who hoped to avoid armed conflict were dismayed.

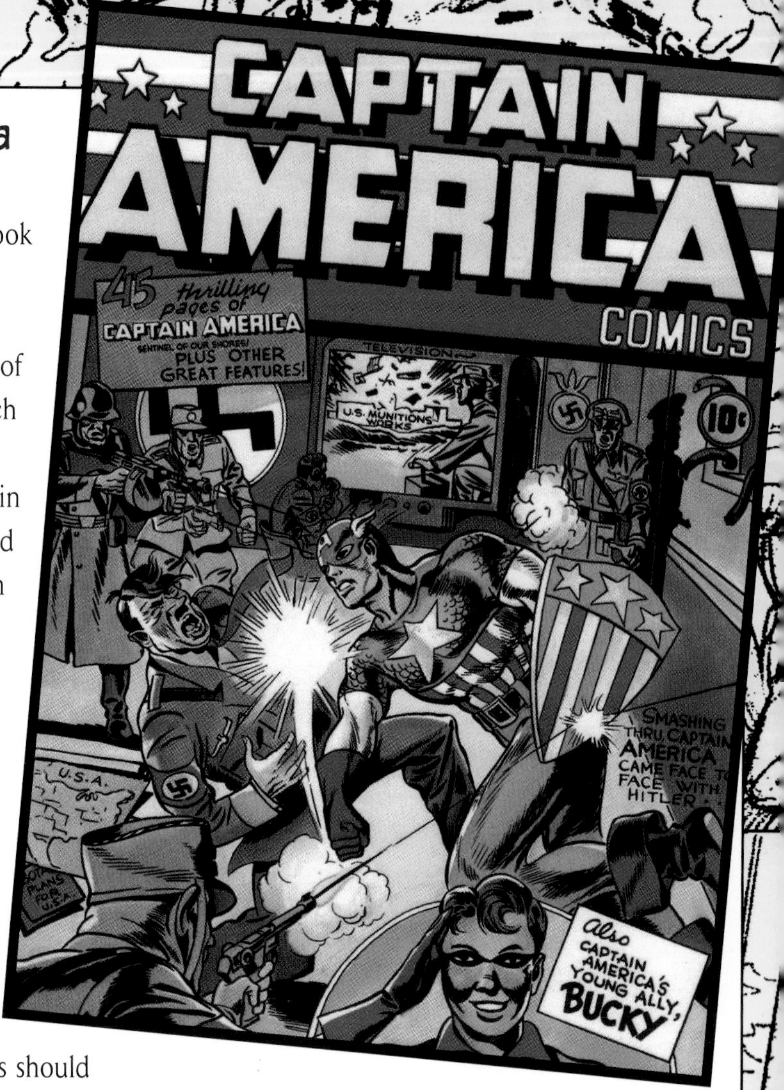
CAPTAIN AMERICA
COMICS
45 thrilling pages of
CAPTAIN AMERICA
SENTINEL OF OUR SHORES!
PLUS OTHER GREAT FEATURES!
TELEVISION
U.S. MUNITIONS WORKS
10¢
SMASHING THRU, CAPTAIN AMERICA CAME FACE TO FACE WITH HITLER...
U.S.A.
also CAPTAIN AMERICA'S YOUNG ALLY, BUCKY

During the war, Captain America became the most popular superhero fighting enemies of the United States. He even had a fan club. A page in each comic invited readers to join the "Sentinels of America." Sometimes the back pages—like others in World War II comics—reminded readers to buy stamps or bonds to help pay for war efforts.

Like other superheroes, Captain America continued appearing in comics after World War II. He fought evil during peacetime, too. And when the United States engaged in other conflicts, he fought the enemy.

Another origin for Captain America?

In 2003 comic book creators Bob Morales and Kyle Baker and editor Axel Alonso re-imagined the origin of Captain America. In their series—titled *Truth: Red, White & Black*—the first Captain America is an African-American named Isaiah Bradley. He and hundreds of other black soldiers are the first ones to try out the U.S. government's experimental, secret "Super Soldier" serum. Only Bradley survives the terrible side effects of the serum long enough to fight the enemy.

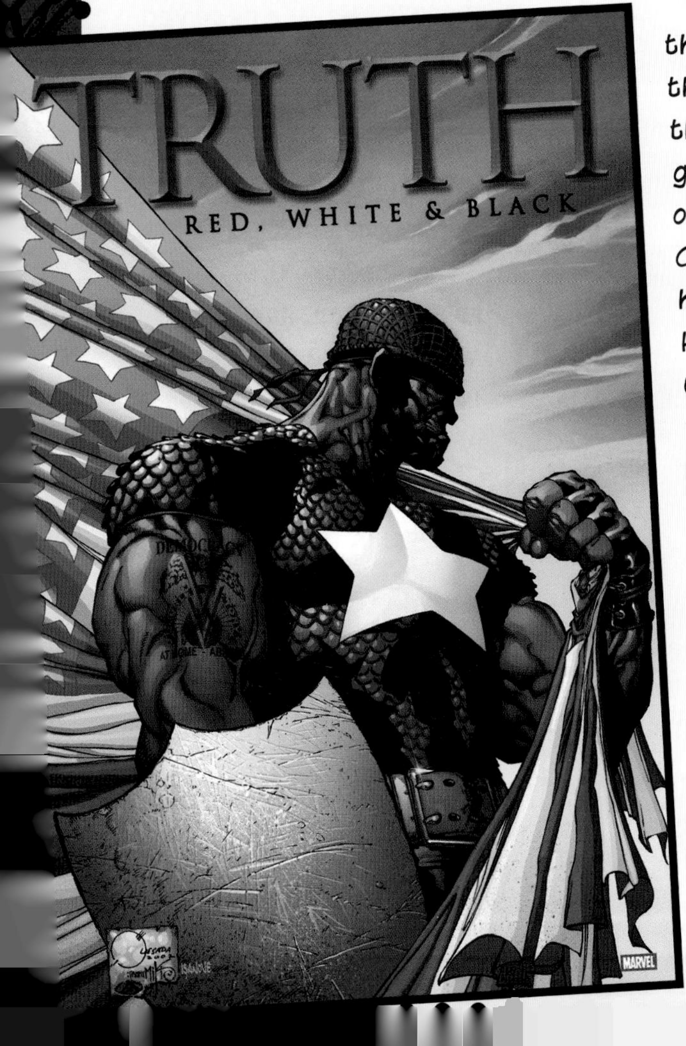
TRUTH
RED, WHITE & BLACK
MARVEL

The top-secret sacrifices of these men produce information that helps scientists perfect the serum. Only then is it given to Steve Rogers, who officially becomes known as Captain America. Alonso and his associates—themselves Hispanic and black—drew upon real-life history as they created this series. From 1932 to 1972, the U.S. government conducted medical experiments on black men in Tuskegee, Alabama. Many suffered and died without receiving treatment while the government continued to gather information. The unethical study came to light when the *Washington Evening Star* exposed the practice in 1972.

Who owns that superhero?

Who owns an idea? In 1938 Jerry Siegel and Joe Shuster sold all rights to Superman to National Allied, the company that became DC Comics. They received just $130 and a contract to produce more Superman stories. Siegel and Shuster later sued the company several times, saying that Superman was their creation. They wanted written credit. They also wanted some of the profits from Superman comics, movies, TV shows, toys, and other merchandise.

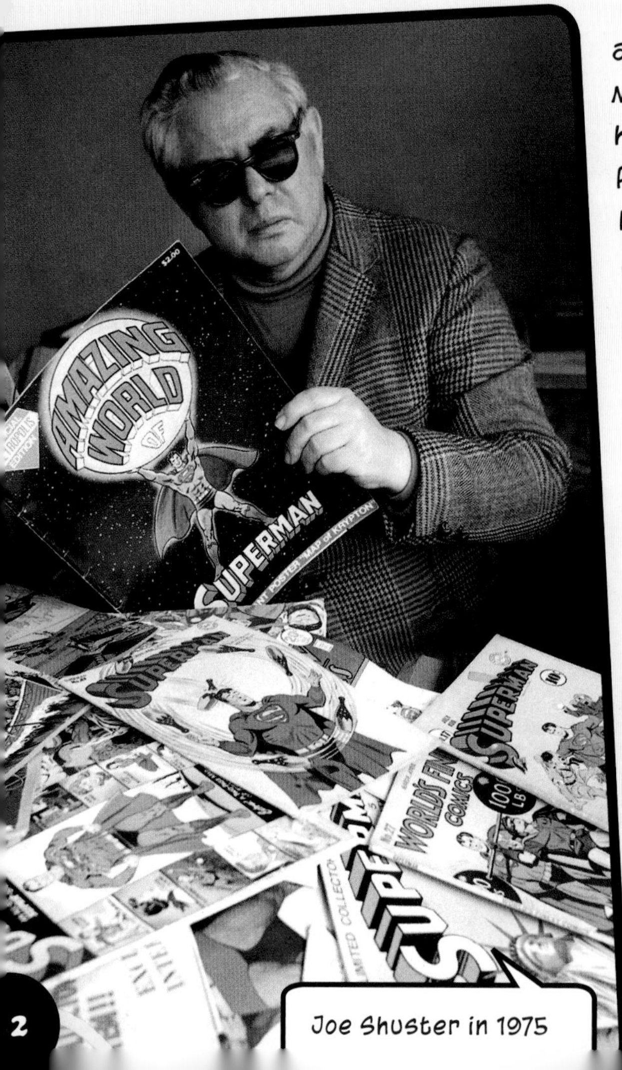
AMAZING WORLD OF
SUPERMAN
$2.00
Joe Shuster in 1975

In 1975 the men received acknowledgment and some money, and in 2008, Siegel's heirs won a major lawsuit. A federal judge ruled that the heirs were entitled to claim a share of the U.S. copyright to Superman. How much money, if any, the heirs will receive remains unsettled.

DC Comics sued the publisher of Captain Marvel in 1951. DC claimed that the superhero was just a "stolen" version of Superman. DC won its court case. In 1972 the company bought the rights to Captain Marvel and began publishing its own Captain Marvel stories under the title *Shazam!*

Teenagers create comics

Many important comic book creators got their start as teens:

* Jerry Siegel and Joe Shuster were both about 19 when they designed Superman.

* Stan Lee—who later created Spider-Man, the Fantastic Four, and Iron Man—began working on comics when he was 17.

* Bob Kane, who later created Batman with writer Bill Finger, was 19 when he drew movie cartoons and 21 when he began drawing comics.

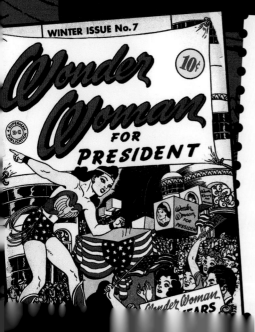

WINTER ISSUE No. 7

10¢

Wonder Woman FOR PRESIDENT

Wonder Woman

The why and how of Wonder Woman

William Moulton Marston (1893–1947) was a psychologist. Unusual for his time, Marston believed women and men had equal abilities. He created the character of Wonder Woman to provide a strong female role model for young readers. Publisher Max Gaines supported this effort.

Hot and cold wars

Comic books showing U.S. soldiers at war flourished during the Korean War (1950–1953). By the time the conflict was over, more than 100 war comics were being published. But some of the most popular titles were ones that looked back at World War II and the Allied victory. *GI Joe* was one such series. It had devoted readers from 1950 until 1957, when it ceased publication. *GI Joe: A Real American Hero* reappeared in the 1980s, in connection with toy action figures.

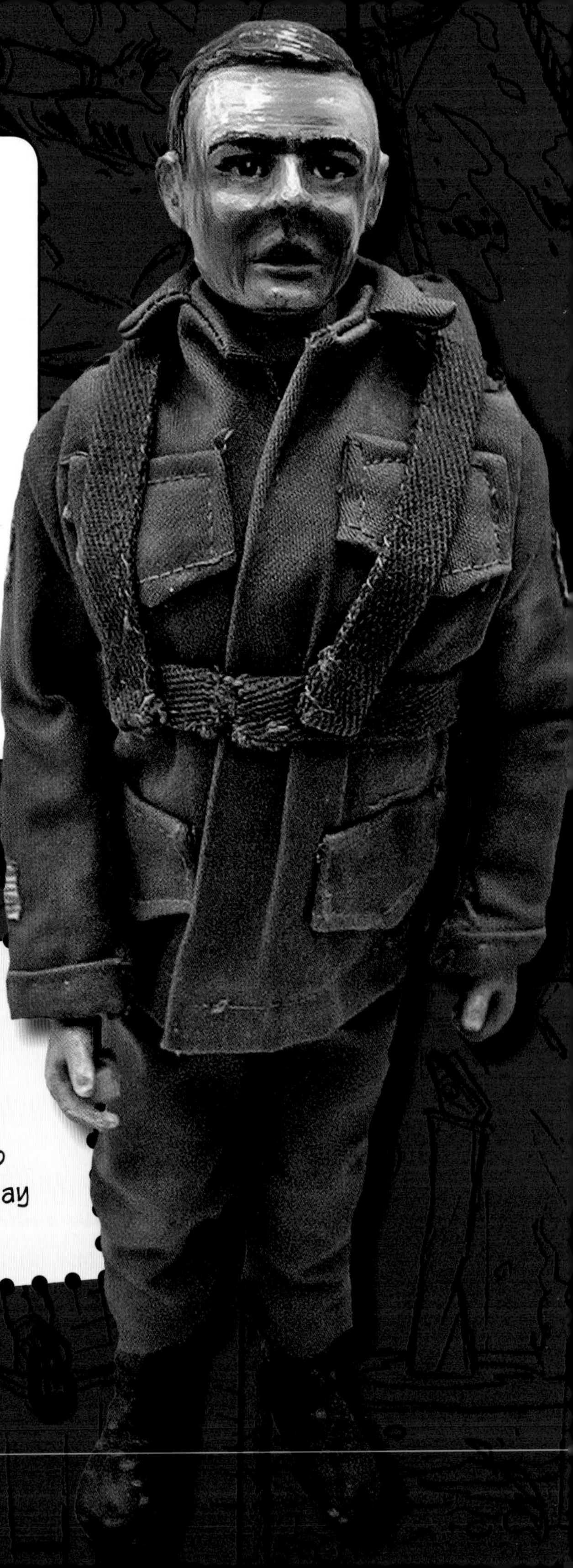

Armed forces comics

The U.S. armed forces often distributed special comic books to troops. The comics were written to instruct soldiers in an enjoyable way about safety and combat topics.

Throughout the 1950s and 1960s, Americans and people in other countries lived with the threat of atomic warfare. Both the United States and its main rival, the Soviet Union, had atomic bombs, which threatened vast destruction. The tension between the countries—known as the Cold War—led to the appearance of a new kind of superhero. The lives of these flawed characters were changed forever by radiation, one of the threats of atomic warfare.

The Thing, a member of the heroic Fantastic Four, was transformed by radiation into a rocklike creature. When people respond to him with fear, he rages: "Maybe I am a monster! I look like one—and sometimes I feel like one! ... If they say I'm a menace, I'll be a menace! I'll show them all!"

The Thing usually keeps his hostile impulses under control, but another comic book character, The Hulk, cannot. An unexpected dose of radiation transforms scientist Bruce Banner into the destructive Hulk whenever Banner becomes angry. In a 1962 comic book, the bite of a radioactive spider transforms teenager Peter Parker into Spider-Man. His everyday problems increase when he has to learn how to use, but still hide, his new superpowers.

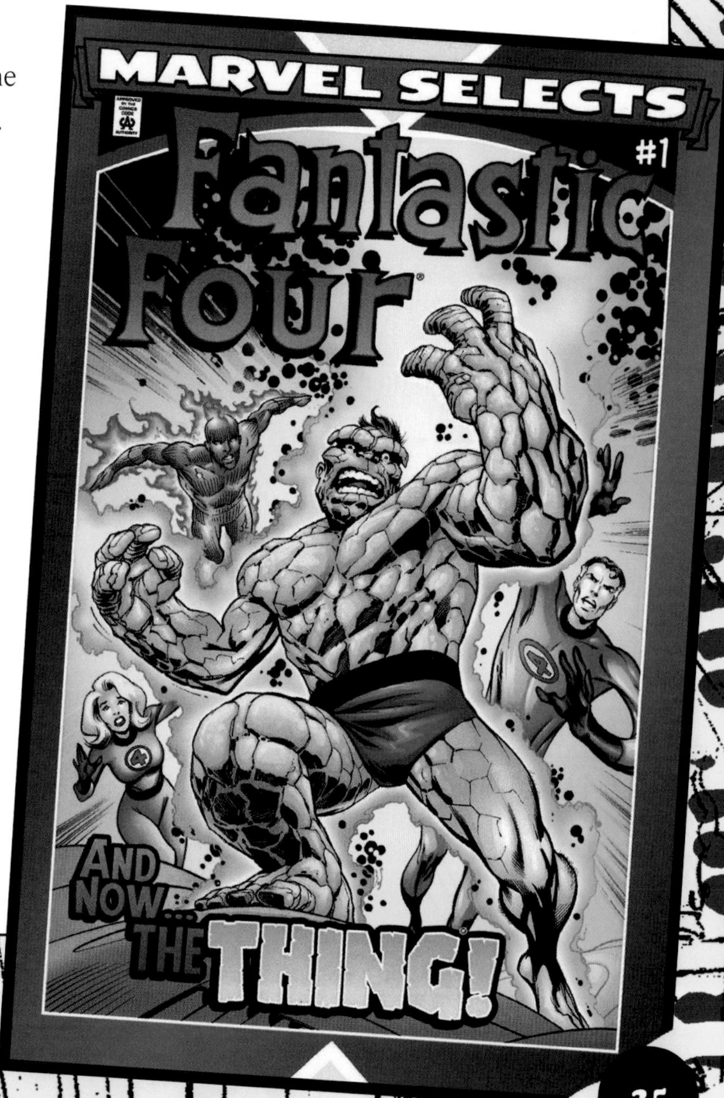
MARVEL SELECTS
Fantastic Four
#1
AND NOW... THE THING!

The Vietnam War

The Vietnam War (1959–1975) stirred controversy worldwide. Many U.S. citizens supported their country's involvement in the conflict, from 1965 to 1973, but many others did not. Comic books reflected these differing views. A new superhero, Iron Man, first appeared in 1963. He fought alongside U.S. soldiers against Communist forces in Vietnam. *Tales of the Green Beret* and *Jungle War Stories* were series that also supported U.S. involvement in the war. One publisher in favor of actively fighting communism included a page titled "Are You Physically Fit?" in each war comic. It urged young men and boys to keep in shape to become better soldiers.

Many other people, though, protested the U.S. military presence in Vietnam. Some wrote letters to publishers, reprinted in the comics themselves, urging that superheroes such as Captain America not appear in Vietnam War stories. One war comic included a pagelong letter supposedly from a soldier fighting in Vietnam. In it he urged his younger brother not to enlist, as he had done.

The 'Nam was a series that looked back at the Vietnam War. Published between 1986 and 1993, it began as an ordinary soldier's view of daily life during combat. By 1993 the series had become less realistic. Its publisher had superheroes entering the fight and had the U.S. winning the war. In reality, the conflict ended with a victory by the North Vietnamese, not the Americans.

Beyond Vietnam

Graphic novels have spotlighted more recent conflicts around the globe. They portray the human costs of such wars. Joe Kubert's *Fax from Sarajevo* follows the life of a family there in the early 1990s, when Serbian forces besieged the city. Mark Stamaty's *Alia's Mission: Saving the Books of Iraq* is set in 2003 in that war-torn country. Both of the graphic novels are based on real events.

The effects of terrorism

The terrorist attacks of September 11, 2001, on the World Trade Center in New York and the Pentagon, near Washington, D.C., inspired a series of special comic books. Several publishers and comic book creators banded together to help survivors and their families. They produced books that honored that day's heroic rescuers and donated the profits of the books to charities aiding survivors. Their views are expressed in a Superman comic. Shown with a fireman holding the American flag, Superman notes that the world is "fortunately protected by heroes of its own."

The cover of one *Spider-Man* issue (volume 2, #36) represented the horror of the September 11 attacks by what it omitted. Except for the words Spider-Man and Marvel Comics, the cover was totally black. This so-called Black Issue indicated that the attacks were beyond describing with words or pictures.

Terrorism, now a more regular threat in many people's lives, has also become a background element in today's comics. Sabra, an Israeli hero in the X-Men comic books, is a woman whose young son was killed by a terrorist attack in her homeland.

Some comic books featuring Captain America have shown the superhero actively responding to terrorist attacks on the United States. In some issues, he has joined U.S. troops in Kandahar, Afghanistan. The "war on terror" began there in 2001. In other comics, Captain America defends Arab-Americans in the United States from violent, unthinking mobs.

CHAPTER 3

Facing the Challenges of Censorship

Critics of comic books have objected to the skimpy clothing and loose morals of some characters in various types of comics, from superhero to romance. Many more critics, though, have objected to the bloodshed and violence in comics.

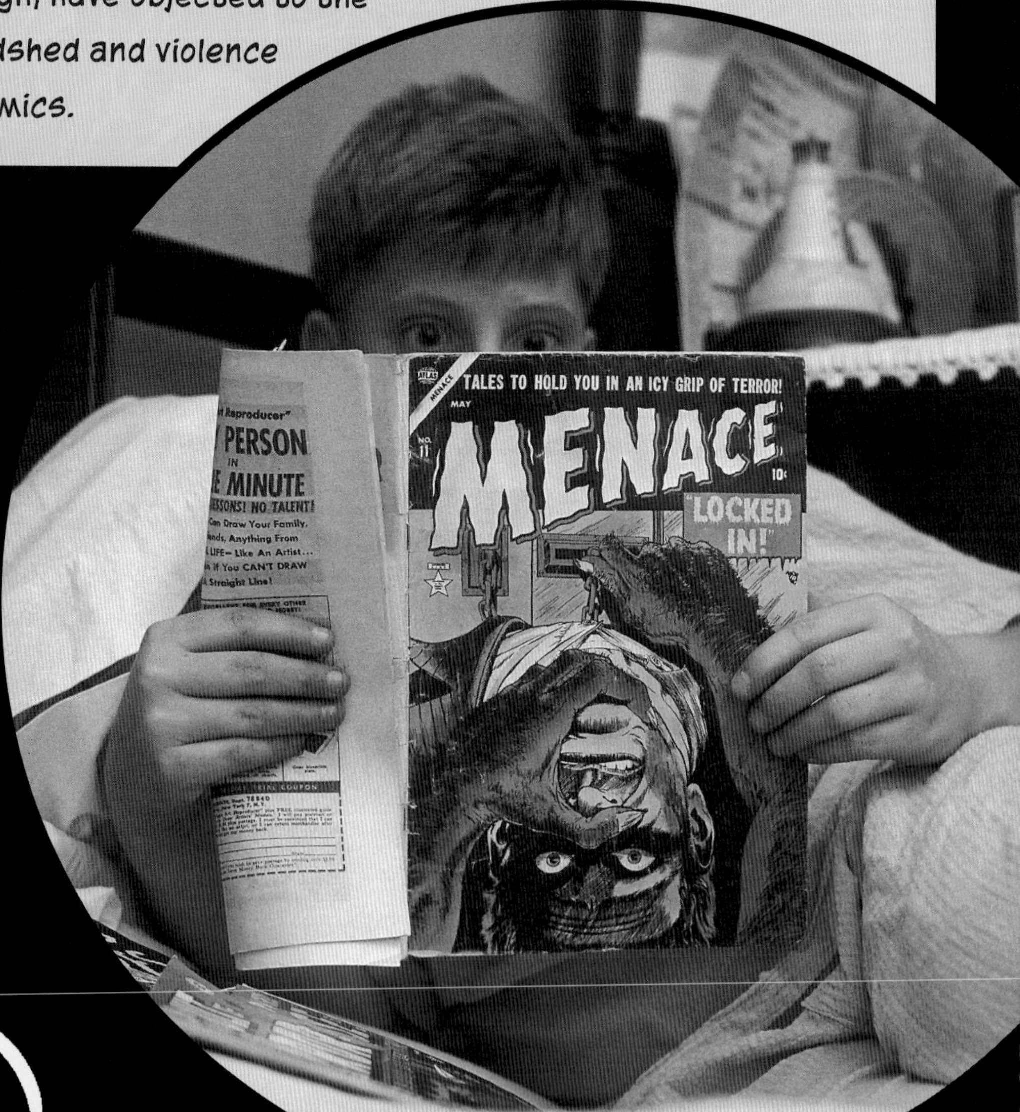
TALES TO HOLD YOU IN AN ICY GRIP OF TERROR!
MENACE
"LOCKED IN!"
PERSON
MINUTE

Horror and crime comics—very popular from the mid-1940s through the mid-1950s—were filled with monstrous behavior, including torture. A horror-comic artist described his work then: "It didn't matter if the story stank and the artwork was rotten as long as it showed a lot of guts hanging out and bloodsucking."

A needle about to be plunged into a terrified woman's eye. A headless body gushing blood. These were just two typical illustrations in these tales.

While supernatural creatures such as vampires and werewolves starred in some horror comics, ordinary people committed much of the violence. Concerned citizens feared that young readers would imitate such behavior.

Some community groups tried to lure kids away from these comics. They offered young readers new hardback books in exchange for their crime or horror comics. Sometimes these swaps worked. In 1955 thousands of comics were collected during Operation Book Swap in Norwich, Connecticut, and Mansfield, Ohio. Other concerned citizens, though, believed stronger actions were needed to combat the "dangers" of comic books.

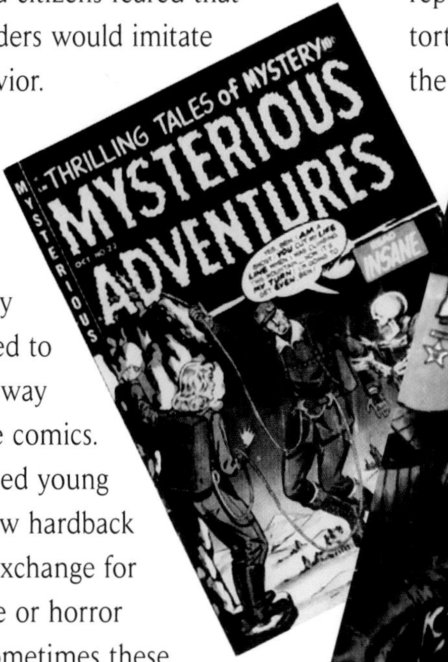
THRILLING TALES OF MYSTERY 10¢
MYSTERIOUS ADVENTURES
MYSTERIOUS

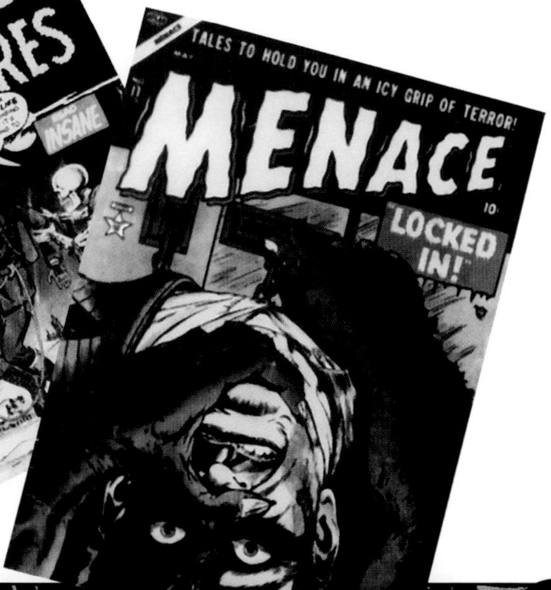
TALES TO HOLD YOU IN AN ICY GRIP OF TERROR!
MENACE
10¢
"LOCKED IN!"

Fueling people's fears

Newspaper stories fueled these people's fears about the bad influence of comics. In 1947, for instance, a newspaper reported the death of a 12-year-old boy who had hanged himself. One of his many comic books had a scene of such a hanging. In 1948 front-page stories reported that three boys ages 6 to 8 had tortured another boy—imitating scenes in the horror comics they all had read.

More wholesome infotainment

U.S. government agencies and businesses have distributed educational comics such as these to kids:

* *Radar, the International Policeman*
* *Adventures in Electricity*
* *The Story of Rubber Heels*
* *Sparky's Second Chance —Fire Safety for Everyone*

How popular do you think these comics were?

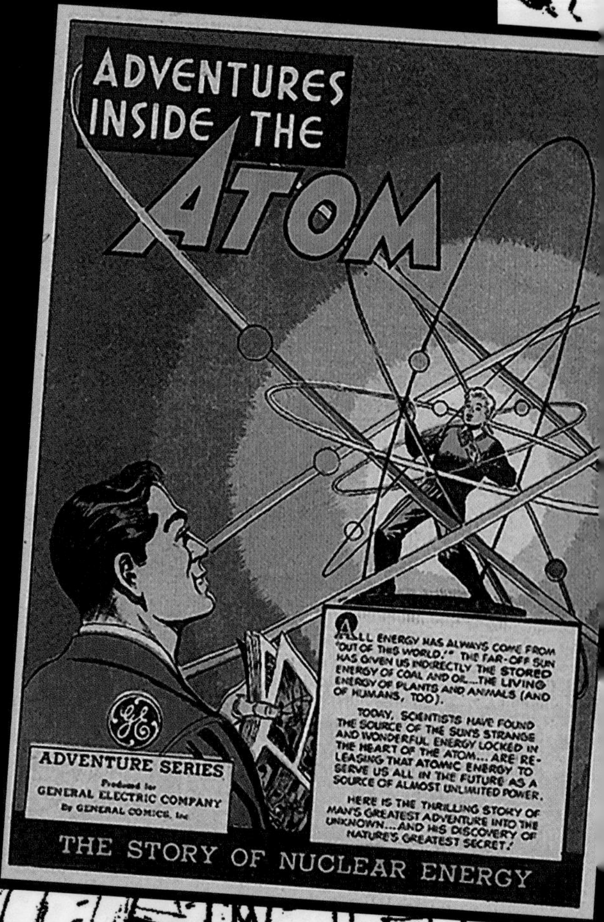
ADVENTURES INSIDE THE ATOM
ALL ENERGY HAS ALWAYS COME FROM "OUT OF THIS WORLD."* THE FAR-OFF SUN HAS GIVEN US INDIRECTLY THE STORED ENERGY OF COAL AND OIL...THE LIVING ENERGY OF PLANTS AND ANIMALS (AND OF HUMANS, TOO).
TODAY, SCIENTISTS HAVE FOUND THE SOURCE OF THE SUN'S STRANGE AND WONDERFUL ENERGY LOCKED IN THE HEART OF THE ATOM... ARE RE-LEASING THAT ATOMIC ENERGY TO SERVE US ALL IN THE FUTURE AS A SOURCE OF ALMOST UNLIMITED POWER.
HERE IS THE THRILLING STORY OF MAN'S GREATEST ADVENTURE INTO THE UNKNOWN...AND HIS DISCOVERY OF NATURE'S GREATEST SECRET!
ADVENTURE SERIES
Produced for GENERAL ELECTRIC COMPANY By GENERAL COMICS, Inc
THE STORY OF NUCLEAR ENERGY

Some critics promoted more wholesome choices. Early in the 1940s, some publishers began producing educational comics in addition to their fun- or excitement-filled best sellers. Series such as *Real Life Comics* and *Real Fact Comics* featured stories about famous people and events in history. Often teachers distributed the comic books in public school classrooms. In some parochial schools, teachers gave students copies of *Treasure Chest Comics,* which were about Catholic saints and historical events. Only the popular *Classics Illustrated* comics, which adapted famous works of literature, sold well alongside adventure-packed or funny comic books.

Banning and burning books

Worried critics banned and even burned some comic books. Parents, community leaders, and church groups tried to get comics they considered offensive removed from store shelves. In 1948 public pressure kept 25 titles off newsstands in Indianapolis, Indiana. That year 36 titles were banned from newsstands and stores in Detroit, Michigan. Around the country, more than 50 cities banned or censored comic books. Pharmacists in New York City agreed that their drugstores would not sell any comics that had not been approved by the National Organization for Decent Literature, which was sponsored by the Catholic Church.

Anxious adults publicly burned piles of these books, sometimes brought in by readers as part of book swaps. In 1945 the public burning of comics was part of Catholic Book Week in some Wisconsin communities. An article in *Time* magazine in 1948 described the burning of offensive comic books in Binghamton, New York. Parents there went door-to-door, collecting comics from each household, and burned them in a large heap as kids stood nearby.

In 1955 the women's auxiliary of the American Legion collected comics for burning in Norwich, Connecticut. Kids could exchange 10 books for a "clean" book.

Seduction of the Innocent

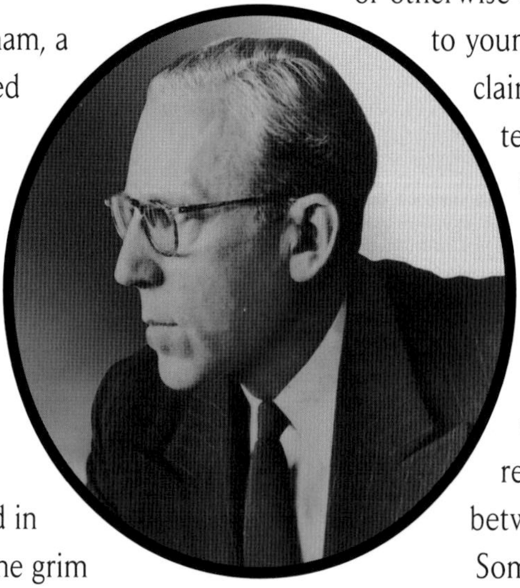

Dr. Frederic Wertham, a psychiatrist who worked with troubled teens, was the leading crusader against the supposed dangers of comics. In the late 1940s, his views on how comics damaged kids' morals and behavior were featured in national magazines. One grim article was titled "Horrors in the Nursery." Wertham titled his own book on the subject *Seduction of the Innocent.* Before the book's 1954 publication, the popular *Ladies' Home Journal* published parts of Wertham's work in six monthly issues.

Wertham insisted that crime, horror, and superhero comics provided dangerous or otherwise improper examples to young readers. He even claimed that Batman and his teenage sidekick, Robin the Boy Wonder, had a romantic relationship! Like many psychiatrists then, Wertham did not approve of any homosexual relationships, let alone one between an adult and a teen. Some people protested that Wertham had incorrectly based his ideas about comics on his work with troubled teenagers. Other opponents claimed that Wertham was prejudiced against homosexuals. Such objections did not lessen the impact of Wertham's remarks. His views led many adults to oppose comics.

Censorship spreads

In the 1940s and 1950s, people in other countries shared Americans' concerns about horror, crime, and superhero comics. People in Ireland, Canada, Australia, New Zealand, Denmark, Norway, Germany, Italy, and the Netherlands campaigned to censor comics. New Zealand banned the sale of all U.S. comics except *Classics Illustrated.* Canada and Great Britain passed laws that punished people for producing or selling comics that contained large amounts of violence and bloodshed.

Laws and regulations

In 1954 and 1955, the U.S. Senate investigated whether—as *Seduction of the Innocent* claimed—comic books led kids to become juvenile delinquents, the term then used for teen lawbreakers. The Senate decided there was some evidence of harmful influence. It recommended that the comic book industry police itself, much as the movie industry had done since the 1930s. A group of publishers formed the Comic Magazine Association of America. They set strict limits on violence and bloodshed and required proper dress and speech for their characters. Comic books that met these standards displayed a seal of approval from the "Comics Code Authority" on their covers. Most stores stopped selling comic books without the seal.

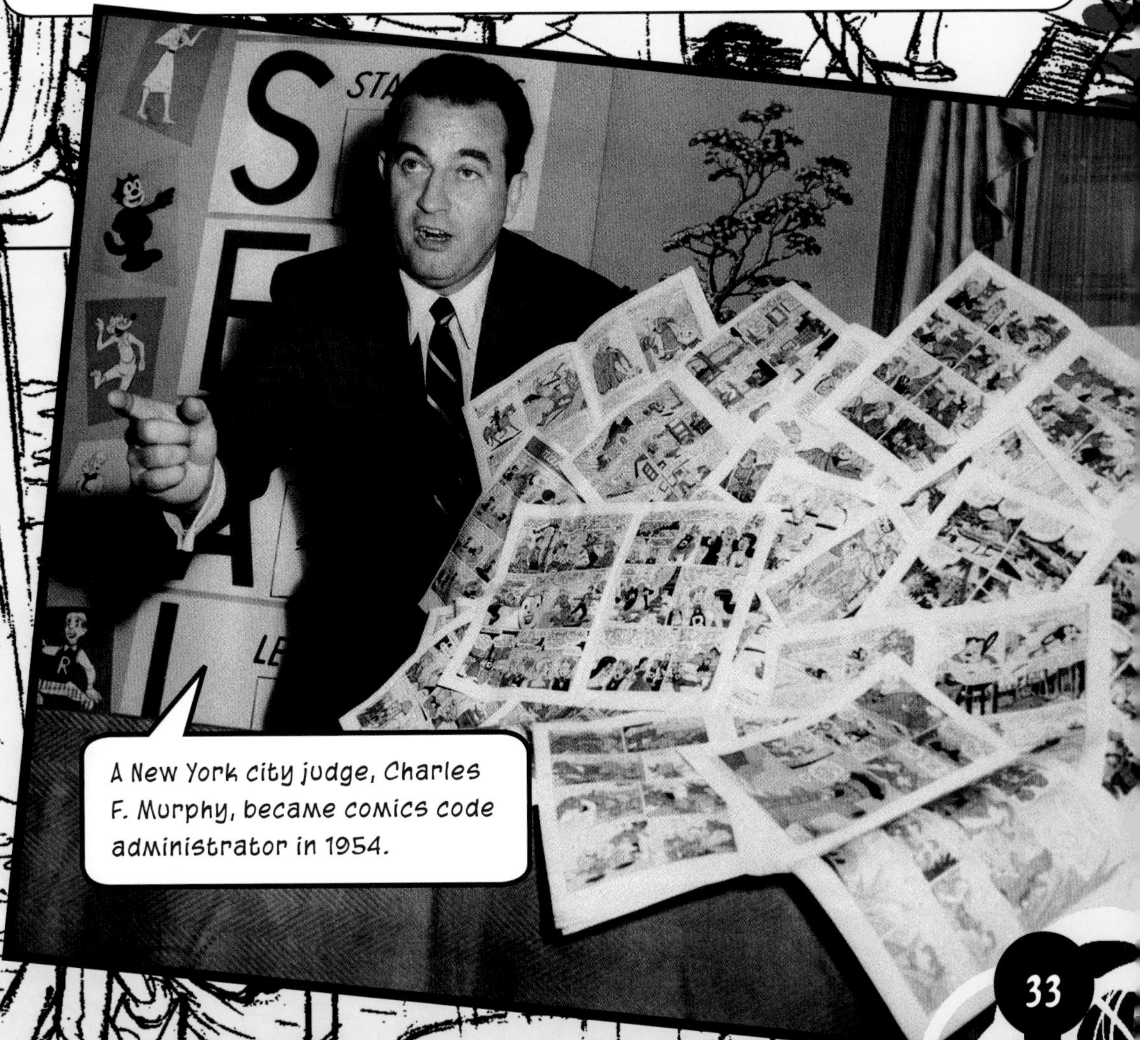

A New York City judge, Charles F. Murphy, became comics code administrator in 1954.

Some publishers changed their comics' stories and pictures to receive the seal of approval. Others went out of business. The censorship changed the shape and size of the comic book industry in the United States. Between 1954 and 1956, the number of comic titles published yearly in the United States dropped from 650 to fewer than 300.

Consequences of censorship

To receive the Comics Code Authority's seal of approval, the creators of war comics toned down the violence of some events they described. The Vietnam-era massacre by American troops at the village of My Lai, for instance, was not shown in all its brutality. Some people who opposed U.S. military involvement in Vietnam believed such censorship harmed their cause.

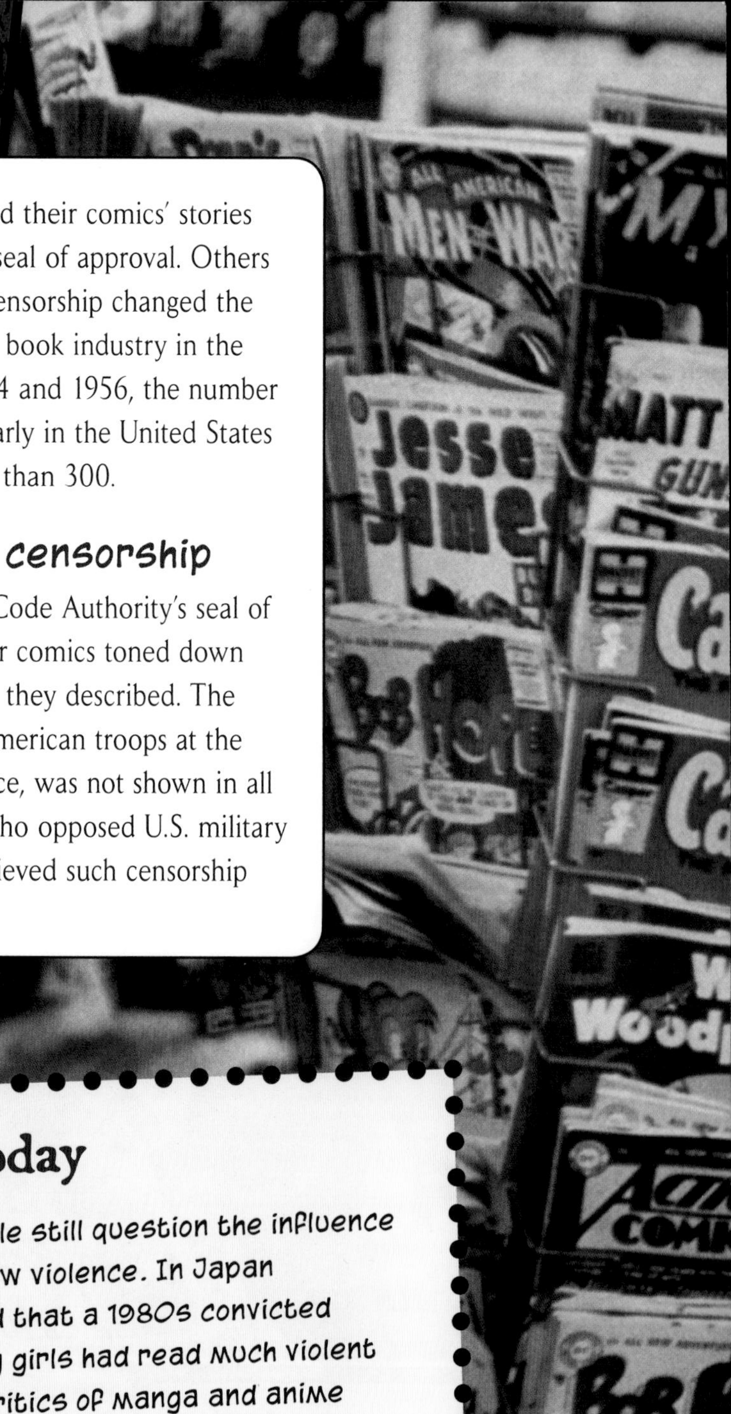

Violence today

Today some people still question the influence of comics that show violence. In Japan newspapers noted that a 1980s convicted murderer of young girls had read much violent manga. In 2007 critics of manga and anime pointed out that a 16-year-old killer had dressed like her favorite cartoon character before attacking her father.

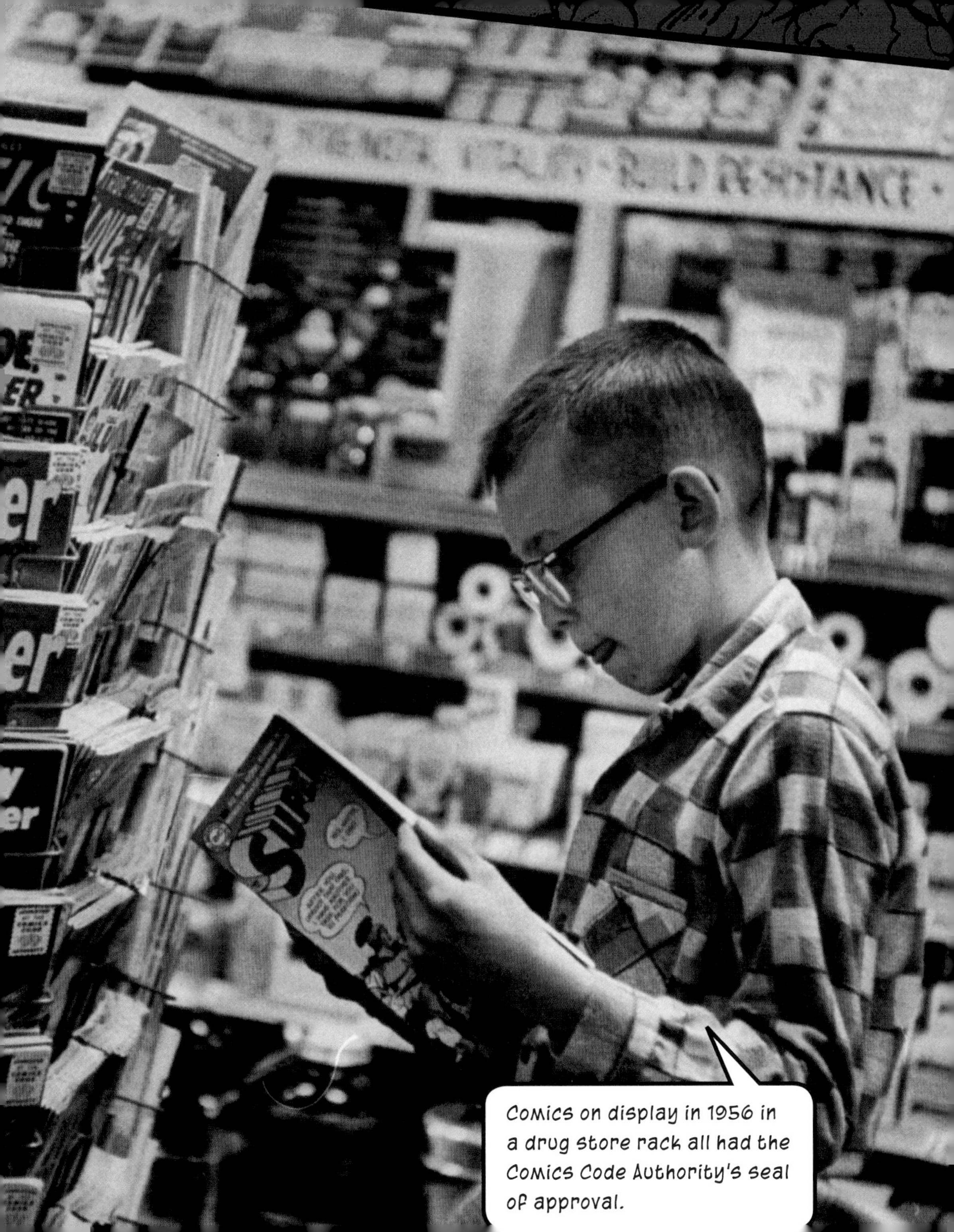

Comics on display in 1956 in a drug store rack all had the Comics Code Authority's seal of approval.

Underground comics

Because certain topics and treatments of ideas did not meet the Comics Code, some independent comic book creators saw an opportunity. A wave of self-published, "underground" comics began in the 1960s. They tackled the counterculture topics of drugs, sexual freedom, and war protests. Some independent publishers grew larger and more successful. Today these publishers continue to offer edgy alternatives to mainstream comic books.

William Gaines and *Mad* magazine

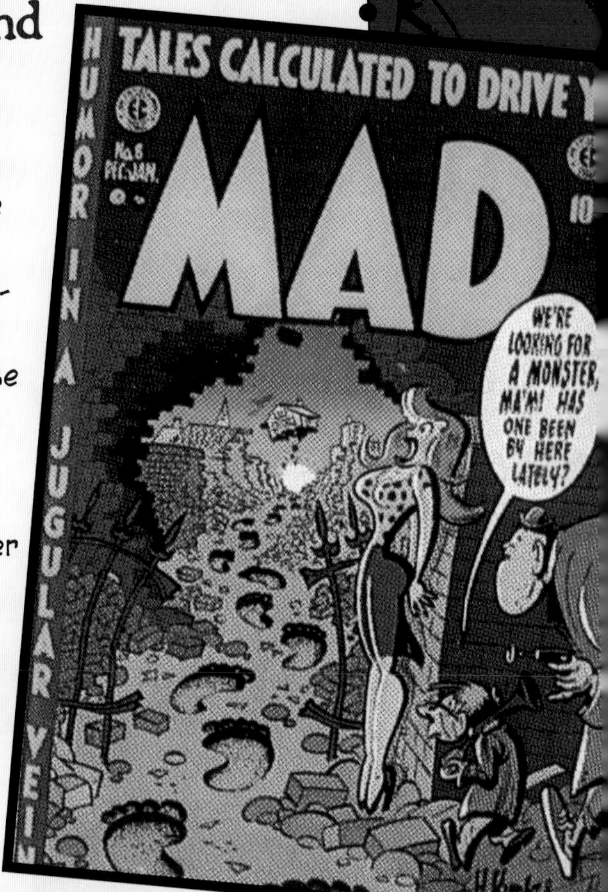
TALES CALCULATED TO DRIVE Y
HUMOR IN A JUGULAR VEIN
MAD
WE'RE LOOKING FOR A MONSTER, MA'M! HAS ONE BEEN BY HERE LATELY?

William Gaines, the publisher of Entertaining Comics and the son of Max Gaines, spoke in defense of comics at the 1954-1955 Senate hearings. He said his comic books did not promote violence or prejudice, another claim made by psychiatrist Frederic Wertham. When several of Gaines' comics later failed to get the Comics Code Authority's seal of approval, Gaines got mad. Really mad. So mad that he transformed one of his humor comics into what became America's most successful monthly humor publication—*Mad* magazine. One of the publication's specialties is spoofing popular comic book characters and stories.

Censorship vs. free speech?

When—if ever—is it right to ban a publication? In 2008 Wal-Mart stores in Texas removed the Mexican comic book *Memin Pinguin* from its shelves. A customer had protested that its central character, a black Cuban boy living in Mexico, is drawn as a monkey. The customer and others said the drawings spread old, prejudiced ideas about black people. Despite frequent objections to the character from Americans, in 2005 Mexico had issued a stamp honoring this popular comic.

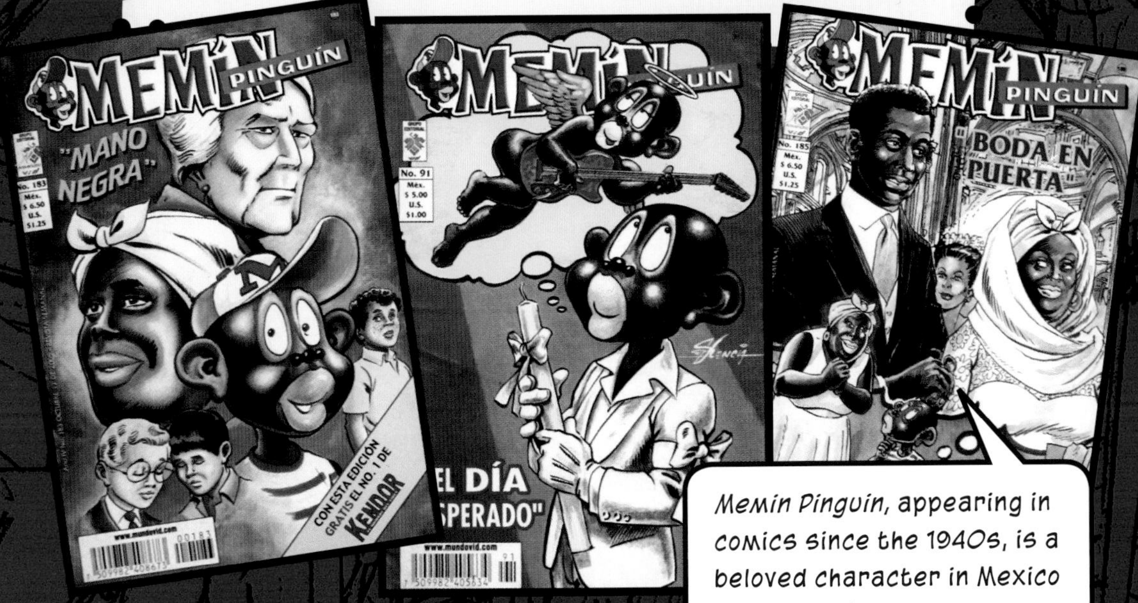

MEMÍN PINGUÍN
"MANO NEGRA"
CON ESTA EDICIÓN GRATIS EL NO. 1 DE KENDOR
MEMÍN
"EL DÍA ESPERADO"
MEMÍN PINGUÍN
"BODA EN PUERTA"

Memin Pinguin, appearing in comics since the 1940s, is a beloved character in Mexico and South America.

Censoring political debate

In 1977 the government of Argentina practiced a deadly form of censorship. Its leaders disapproved of comic book creator Hector Oesterheld, whose comic book biography of rebel Che Guevara and other works criticized the government. Like many other opponents of the military dictatorship, Oesterheld was seized, denied a trial, and killed.

CHAPTER 4

Facing the Challenges of Social Change

Comic books have often mirrored social issues of their day. During the hard economic times of the Great Depression in the 1930s, reading about superheroes allowed readers to feel powerful and in control.

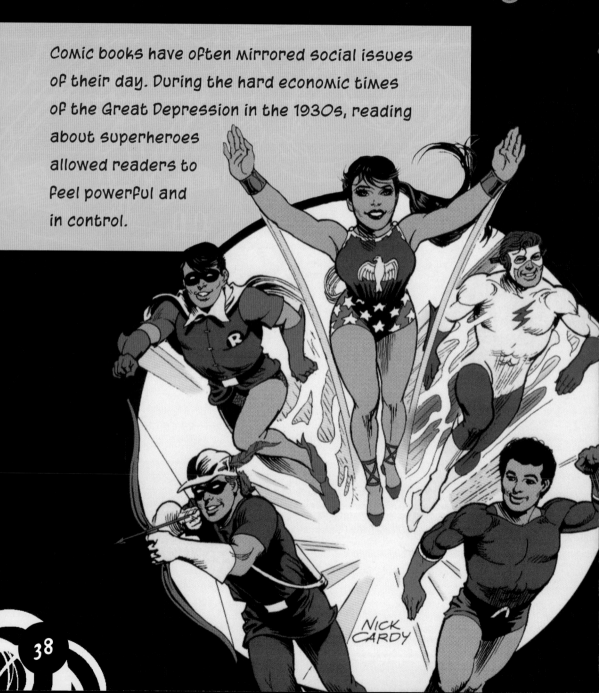

NICK CARDY

Comic book fan and creator Jules Feiffer recalled his poor boyhood during the Depression. He said:

Nice guys finished last; landlords, first. Villains … were miles ahead. It was not to be believed that any ordinary human being could combat them. More was required. Someone with a call. When Superman at last appeared, he brought with him … deep satisfaction.

It is no surprise, then, that superheroes changed when society did. Since many teens in the better economic times of the 1960s and 1970s had more money to spend on comics, publishers added more teen superheroes to their tales.

Marvel Comics' teenage Spider-Man was a hero himself, not just a sidekick. DC Comics debuted a league of young superheroes called the Teen Titans. The Legion of Superheroes was another group that worked alongside famous teenage superhero Superboy. They came from the future to aid their present-day counterparts.

Confronting problems

These super teens, along with adult superheroes in this period, called the Silver Age of Comics, faced problems different from those of the 1930s and 1940s—the so-called Golden Age. Besides questions about the Vietnam War, the 1960s and 1970s brought demands for equal rights for minorities, women, and homosexuals. Americans confronted the issues of illegal drug use, government corruption, and damage to the environment. These concerns surfaced in comic books as the Comics Code Authority relaxed its rules.

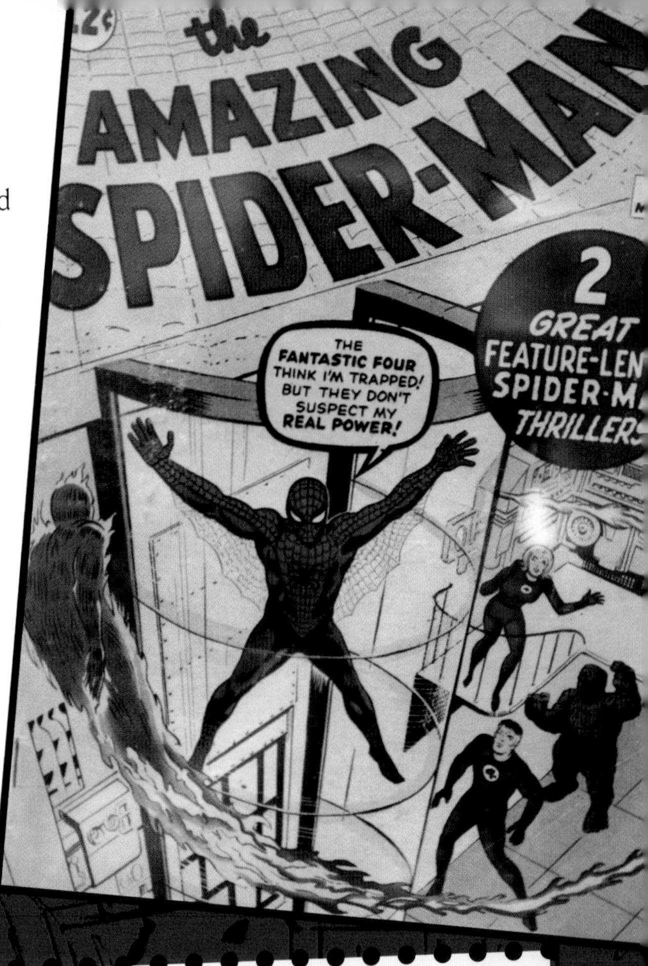
the AMAZING SPIDER-MAN
THE FANTASTIC FOUR THINK I'M TRAPPED! BUT THEY DON'T SUSPECT MY REAL POWER!
2 GREAT FEATURE-LEN SPIDER-M THRILLERS

Defying the Comics Code Authority

In 1971 Stan Lee and Marvel Comics defied the Comics Code Authority to produce three Spider-Man stories about the evils of drug abuse. Even though the U.S. Department of Health, Education, and Welfare had asked Lee to create these comics, the CCA did not give them its seal of approval. It had forbidden any mention of drugs. Controversy about its refusal eventually led the authority to relax its rules.

Teen superheroes

Some teen superheroes from the future had strange superpowers. Their heroic names are clues to their special abilities. Can you figure out the superpower of each of these characters?

* Triplicate Girl
* Phantom Girl
* Cosmic Boy
* Bouncing Boy
* Ferro Lad
* Beast Boy

Search online or at a library and then check your answers on page 61.

In a 1960s comic, the green Hulk sympathizes with a black teenager, saying, "World hates us ... both of us! ... Because we're different!" In 1966 Marvel Comics introduced the first major black superhero, Black Panther, an African prince. Three years later, it introduced the first black American superhero, the Falcon. In a 1970 issue of the *Lois Lane* comic, Lois borrows alien technology from Superman to become a black woman. She then painfully learns firsthand what it means to be African-American in Metropolis. In the 1990s, a group of black comic book creators formed Milestone Media, which featured new black superheroes, such as Icon and teenager Static.

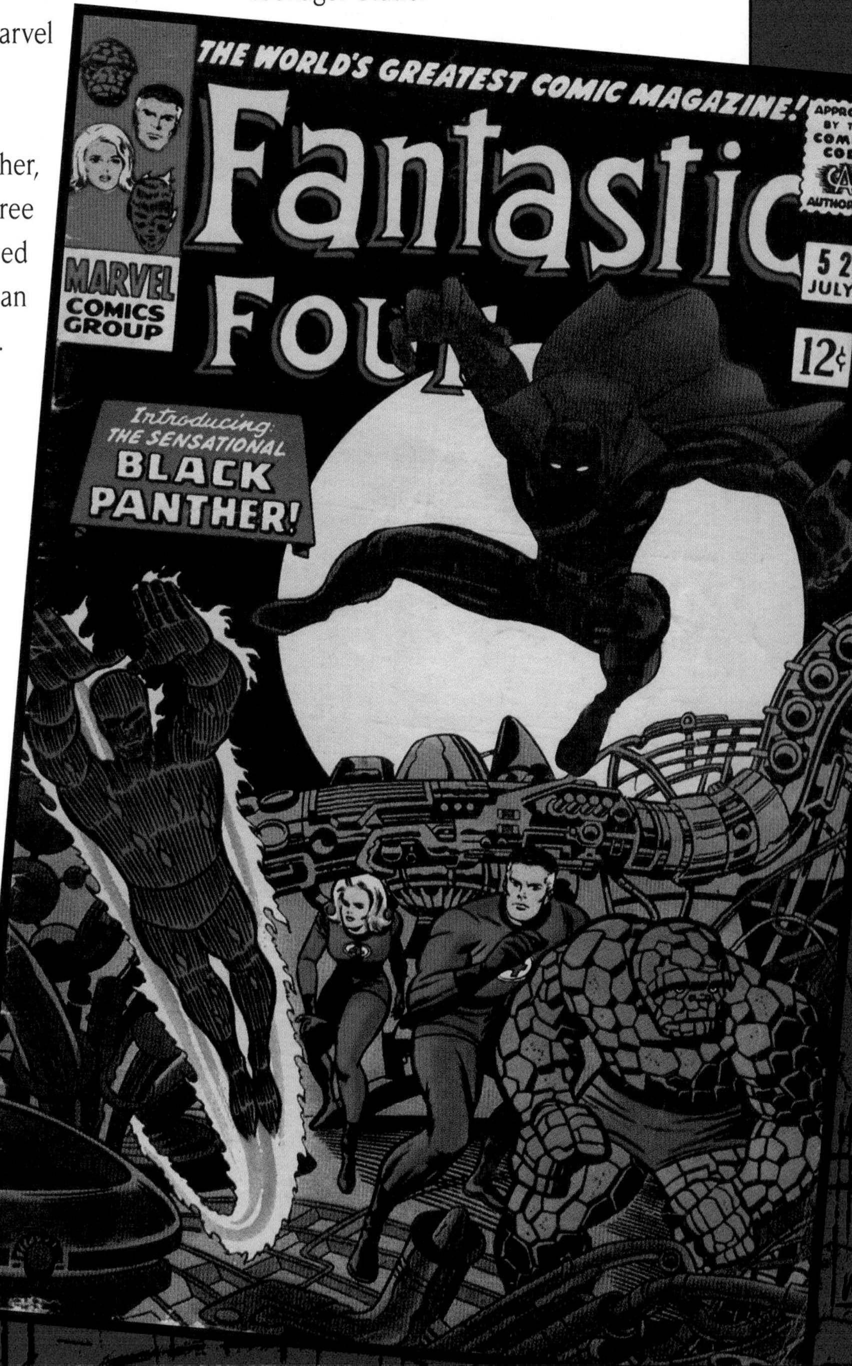
THE WORLD'S GREATEST COMIC MAGAZINE!
Fantastic
FOU
MARVEL
COMICS
GROUP
52
JULY
12¢
Introducing:
THE SENSATIONAL
BLACK
PANTHER!

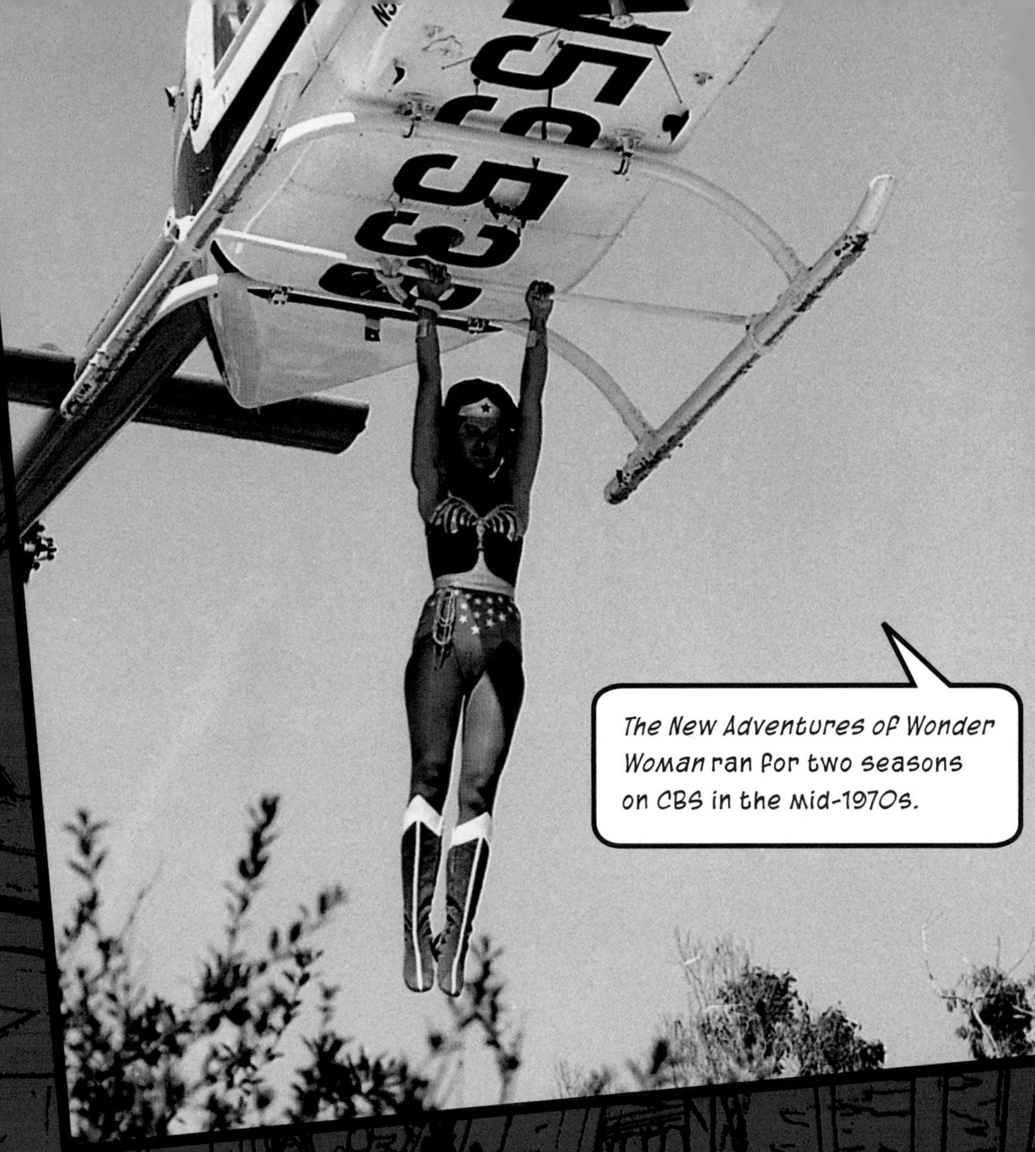

The New Adventures of Wonder Woman ran for two seasons on CBS in the mid-1970s.

In the *Green Lantern/Green Arrow* series, Green Arrow helps the less aware Green Lantern to understand social problems and people's efforts to solve them. In 1992 Marvel Comics revealed that one of its longtime superheroes, Northstar, was gay. In later issues, Marvel tackled the issue again by publishing fan letters about Northstar's sexual identity. In other comics, Iron Man began to fight poverty, injustice, and pollution in the United States. More female superheroes appeared in comics, and heightened interest in female characters led to a *Wonder Woman* TV series in 1975.

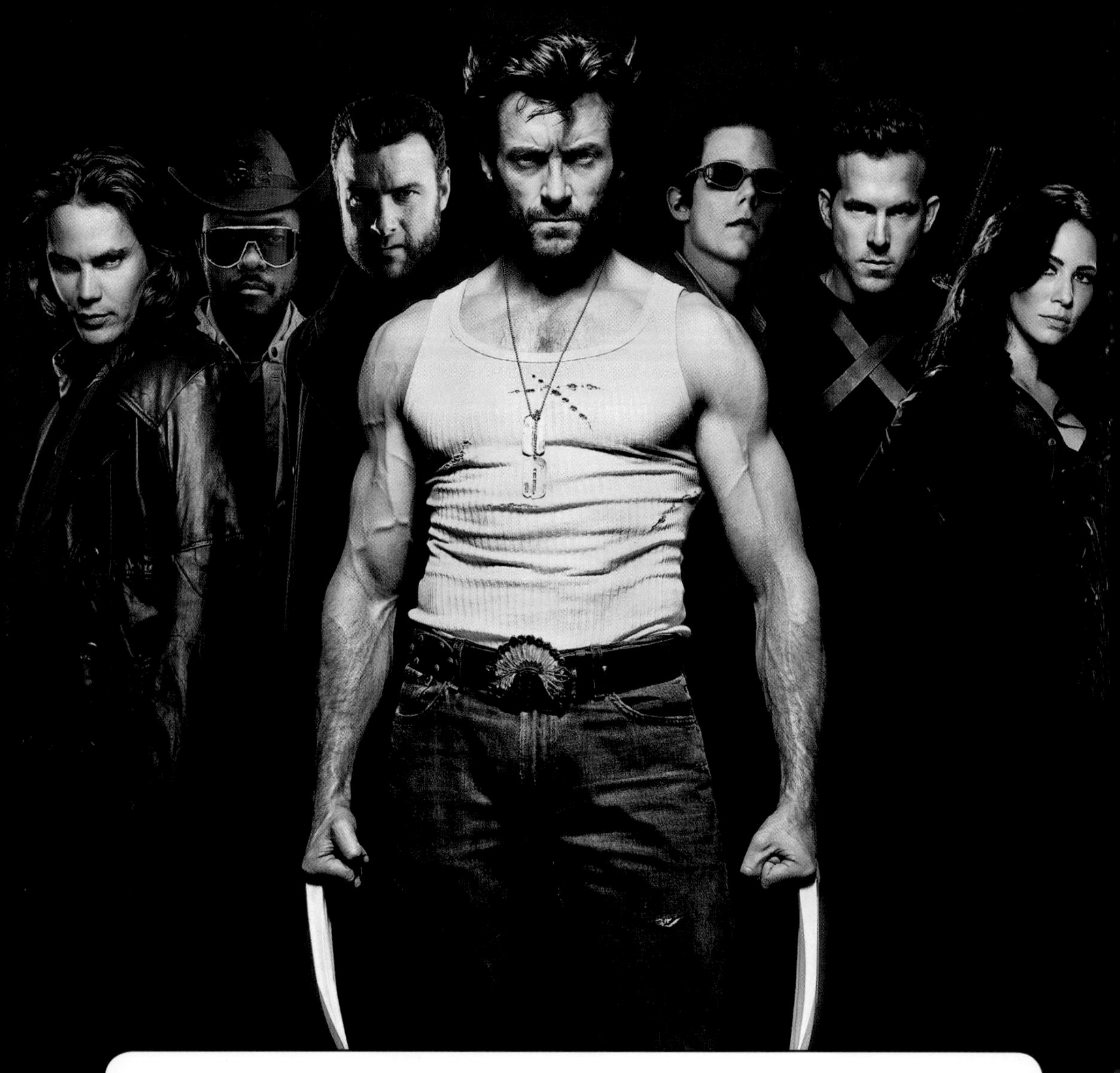

The ultimate outsiders

A group of superheroes—Marvel Comics' X-Men—created in 1963 by Stan Lee are the ultimate outsiders. These mutant humans experience discrimination because other people fear or are repelled by their differences. In this way, the X-Men and other mutants, despite their special powers, are just like any other minority group. Their responses to discrimination also reflect real-life disagreements. The leader of the X-Men, Professor Xavier, wants to work within society while Magneto, who leads an opposing band of mutants, wants a revolution. Their views parallel the differences between black civil rights leaders Martin Luther King Jr. and Malcolm X.

Will Eisner, godfather of American comics

U.S. comic book creator Will Eisner influenced comics for seven decades. His superhero *The Spirit* first appeared in newspaper strips in 1941 and comic books in 1942. The crime fighter protected people on city streets that resembled those in Eisner's own working-class New York. A movie version of *The Spirit* opened in 2008.

Eisner taught and wrote about comics. He is credited with creating the first graphic novel in 1978. Titled *A Contract With God*, this powerful book about loss and anger is also set in a working-class New York City neighborhood. The U.S. comic book industry honored Will Eisner's many achievements by naming its yearly awards the Eisner Awards.

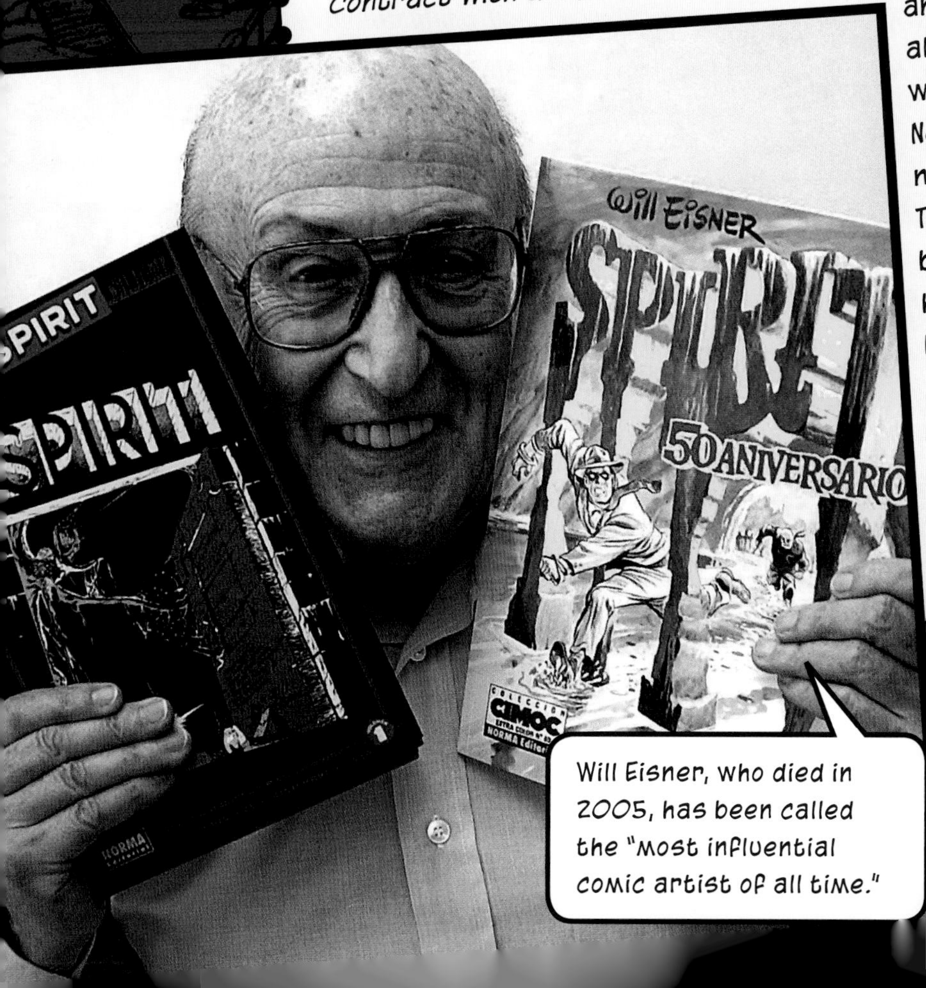
SPIRIT
SPIRIT
WILL EISNER
SPIRIT
50 ANIVERSARIO

Will Eisner, who died in 2005, has been called the "most influential comic artist of all time."

Comic books in other forms

Comic books have a long history of being presented in other forms, using the latest technology. Superman was a character in early radio shows, a 1940s series of theatrical animated shorts, 1940s movie serials, and a 1950s TV series. He's around today in Superman movies and the *Smallville* television series.

In the 1960s, a joke-filled TV series about Batman was popular. Since then several movies based on this superhero and others—such as the Fantastic Four and Iron Man—have appeared.

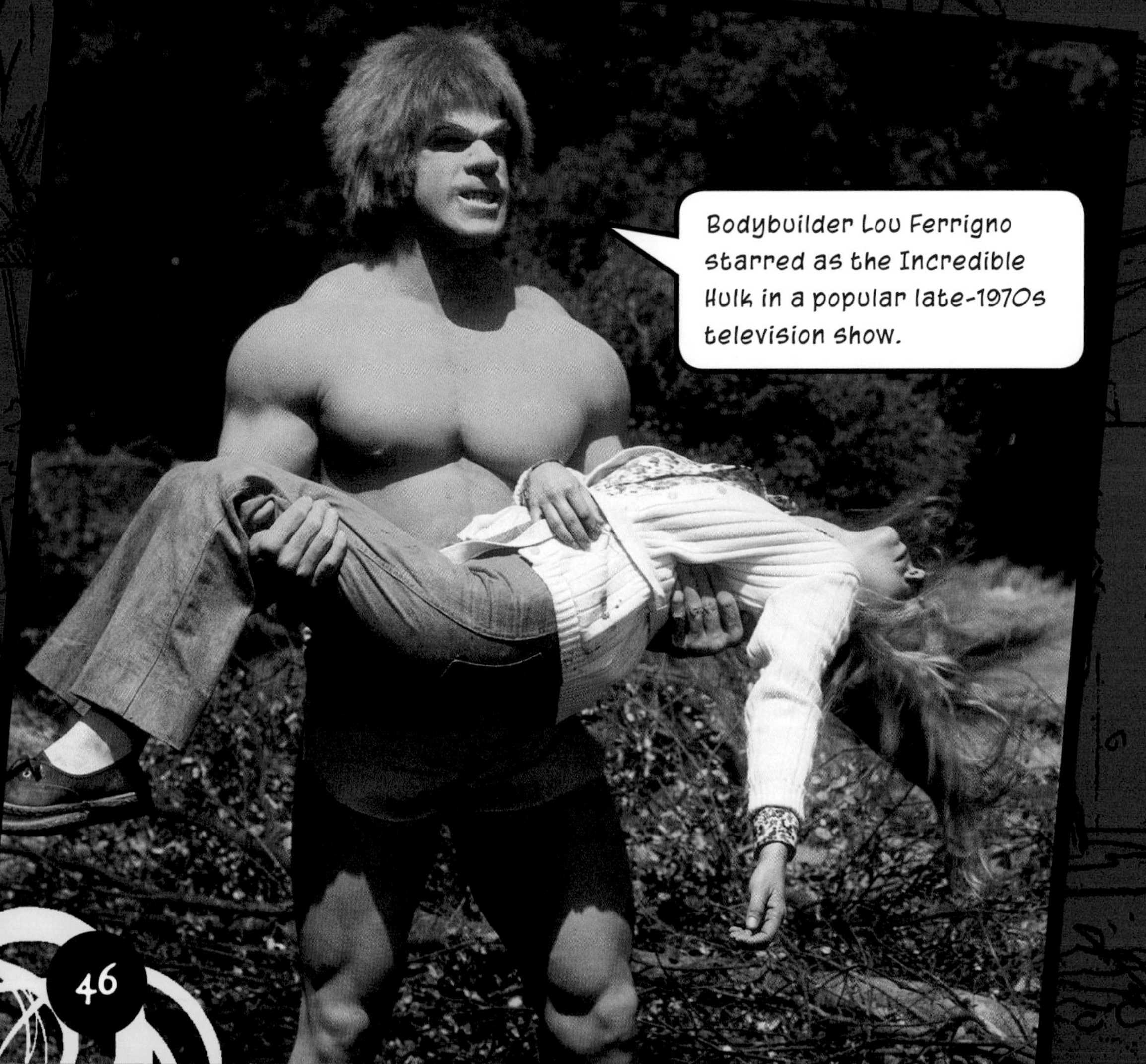

Bodybuilder Lou Ferrigno starred as the Incredible Hulk in a popular late-1970s television show.

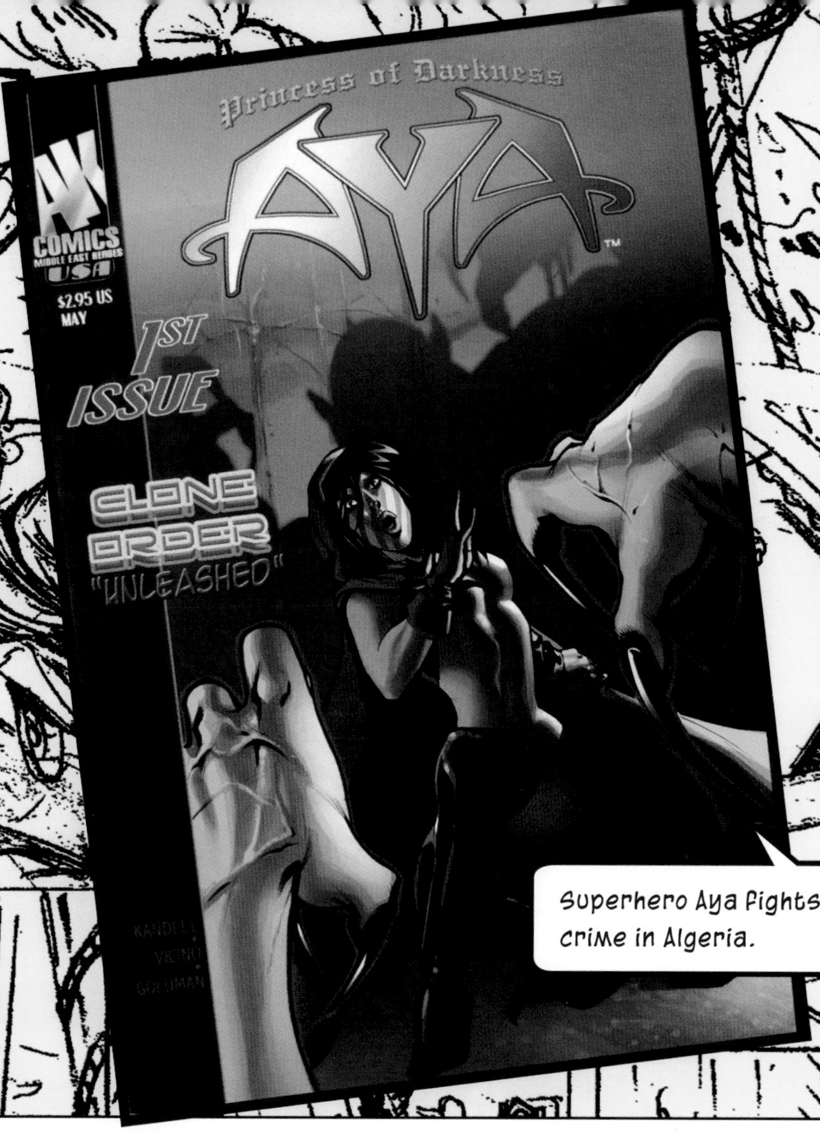
Princess of Darkness
AYA
AK
COMICS
MIDDLE EAST HEROES
USA
$2.95 US
MAY
1ST
ISSUE
CLONE
ORDER
"UNLEASHED"
KANDELL
VICINO
GOLDMAN

Superhero Aya fights crime in Algeria.

Around the globe

Superheroes aren't just Americans. AK Comics, based in Egypt, features Zein, the last Pharaoh, who uses ancient technology and is superstrong, and Jalila, a scientist who gained her superpowers through radiation. In Nigeria Powerman had abilities much like Superman's. Comic books around the globe, however, do more than address such social problems as crime. In India comic book creator and publisher Anant Pai produces comic books that help keep Indian legends and religion alive. He helps to preserve his nation's identity this way. In South Africa and Tanzania, comic books sponsored by the government and international organizations teach people ways to stay healthy. It is Japan's comic books, however, that rival and often surpass U.S. comics as the major force in comics worldwide.

World politics and comics

Social change occurs among countries as well as within them. New nations develop and older ones, such as China and India, become more advanced in technology and industry. Once the world's most powerful country, the United States is today just one powerful country among many. The situation is mirrored in the global culture of comic books.

Japanese comic books, called manga, influence comic book creators in many countries, especially China and South Korea. The style, quality, variety, and number of Japanese comic books make them influential. Forty percent of all books published in Japan are manga.

Translated Japanese manga now occupy whole bookshelves in U.S. bookstores—a development that began in the 1980s. Rapid changes in technology have further increased their presence.

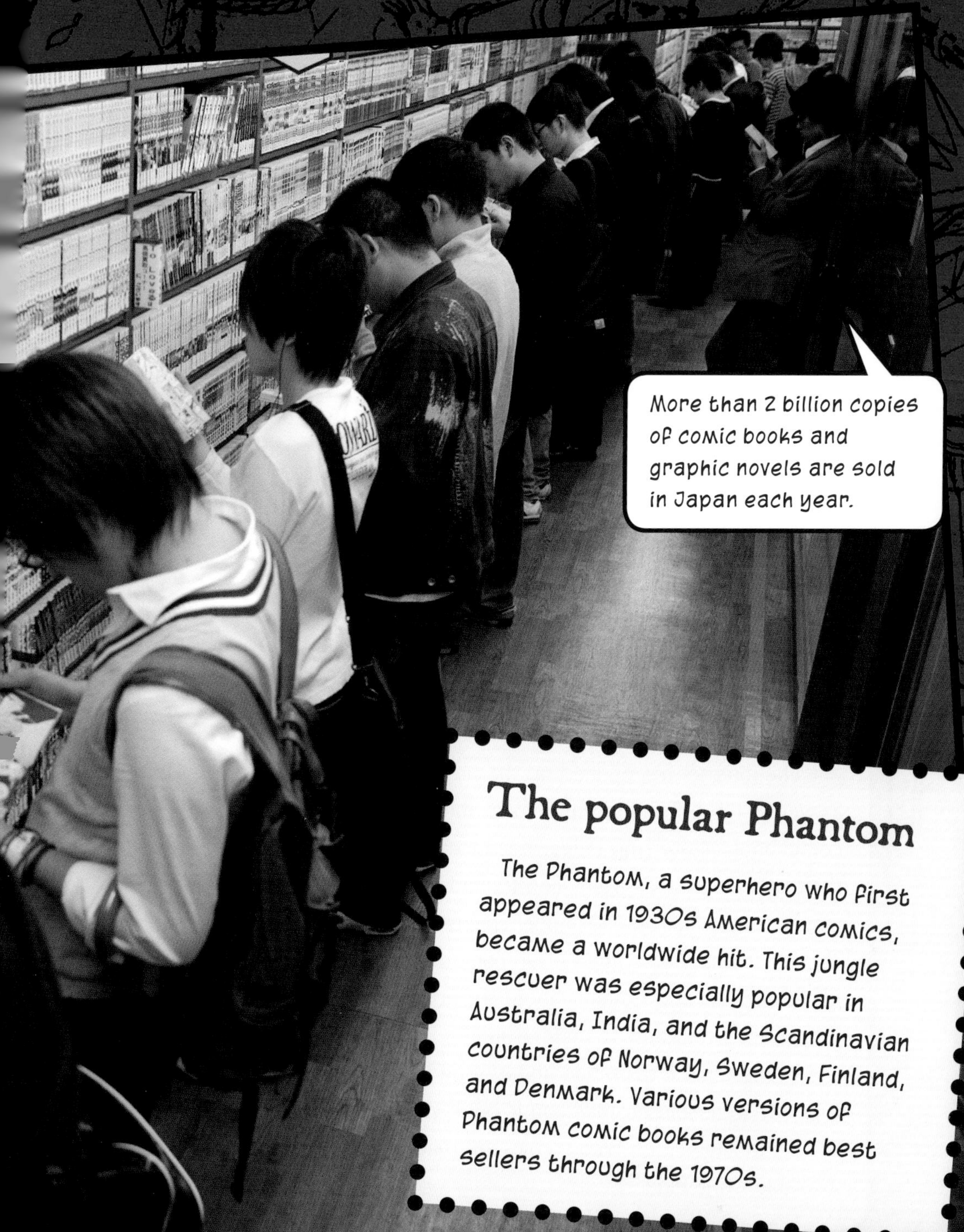

More than 2 billion copies of comic books and graphic novels are sold in Japan each year.

The popular Phantom

The Phantom, a superhero who first appeared in 1930s American comics, became a worldwide hit. This jungle rescuer was especially popular in Australia, India, and the Scandinavian countries of Norway, Sweden, Finland, and Denmark. Various versions of Phantom comic books remained best sellers through the 1970s.

Comics and technology

In addition to bookstores and libraries, comics can now be found online. Scanlations of Japanese manga are just one kind of comic available there. Scanlations are comics that have been translated into English and can be downloaded with their scanned images, hence their name. The Internet also provides a place where fans can discuss manga and other comics in blogs and user groups. There are more than 1,400 Web sites devoted just to manga.

In Japan some comic book fans now have new episodes of their favorite manga sent directly to their cell phones. Of course new video games and anime continue to be developed.

Techno changes

The Internet has opened up the production as well as the distribution of comics. Independent comic book creators no longer need to produce their works on paper. Many comics and even graphic novels are posted online, chapter by chapter. These Web comics often contain the new ideas and critical comments about society that once were found only in underground comics of the 1960s and 1970s. While underground comics typically were sold in small comic book stores, usually in large cities, Web comics are readily available worldwide.

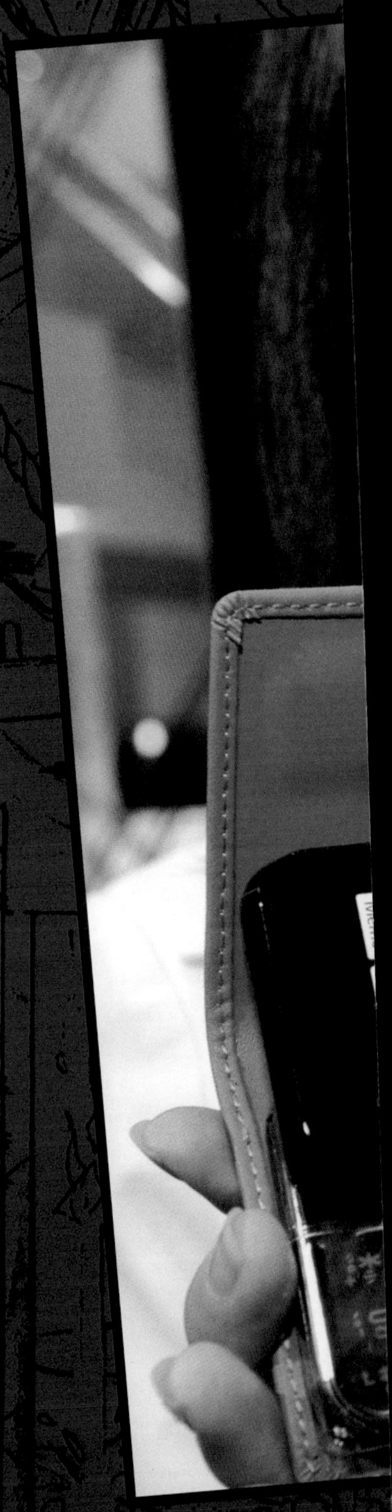

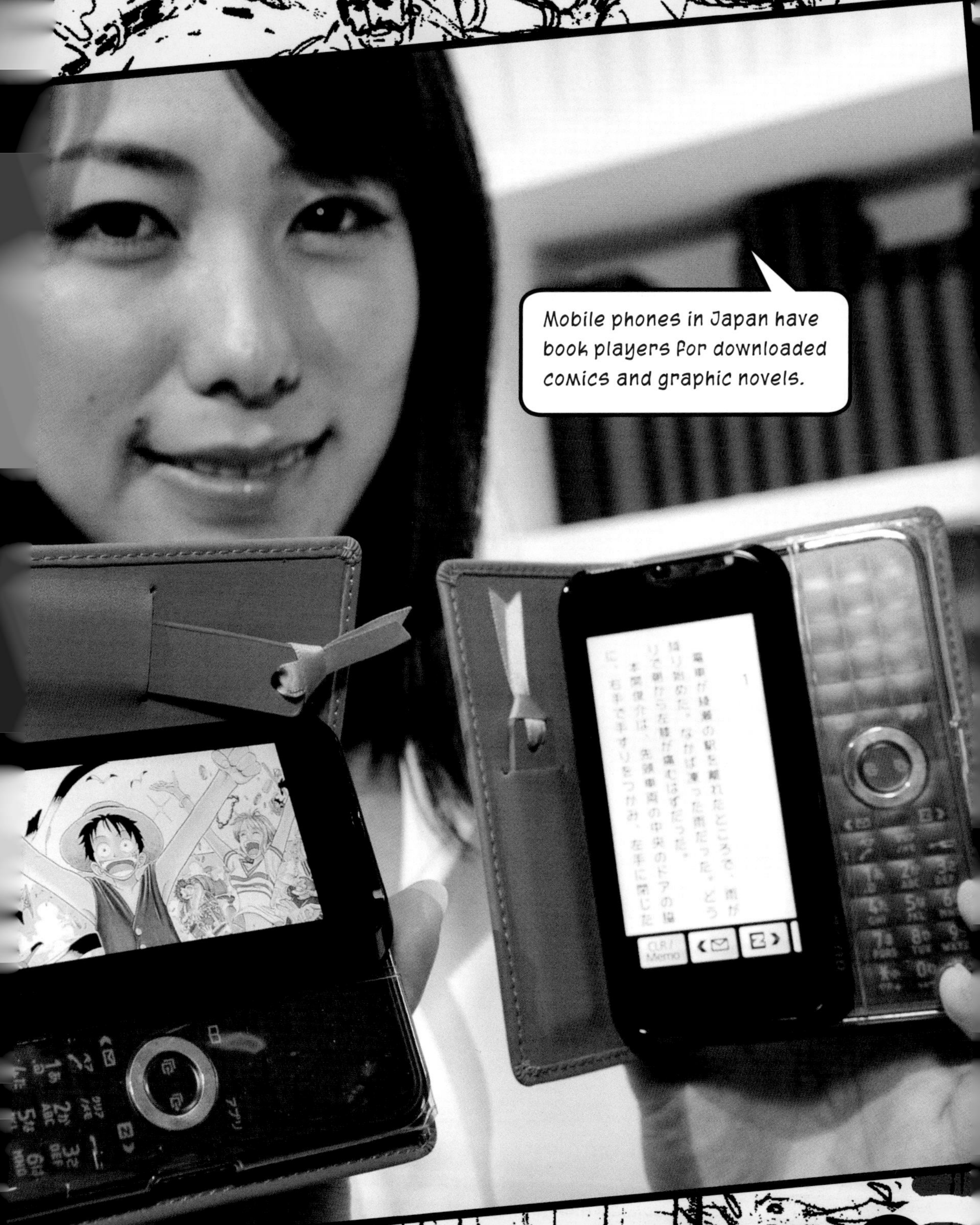

Mobile phones in Japan have book players for downloaded comics and graphic novels.

CHAPTER 5

Out of the Shadows

Today comic books have emerged from the shadows of social scorn. Once considered of interest only to children, and later thought to be not decent enough for children, comics have become major business and cultural successes.

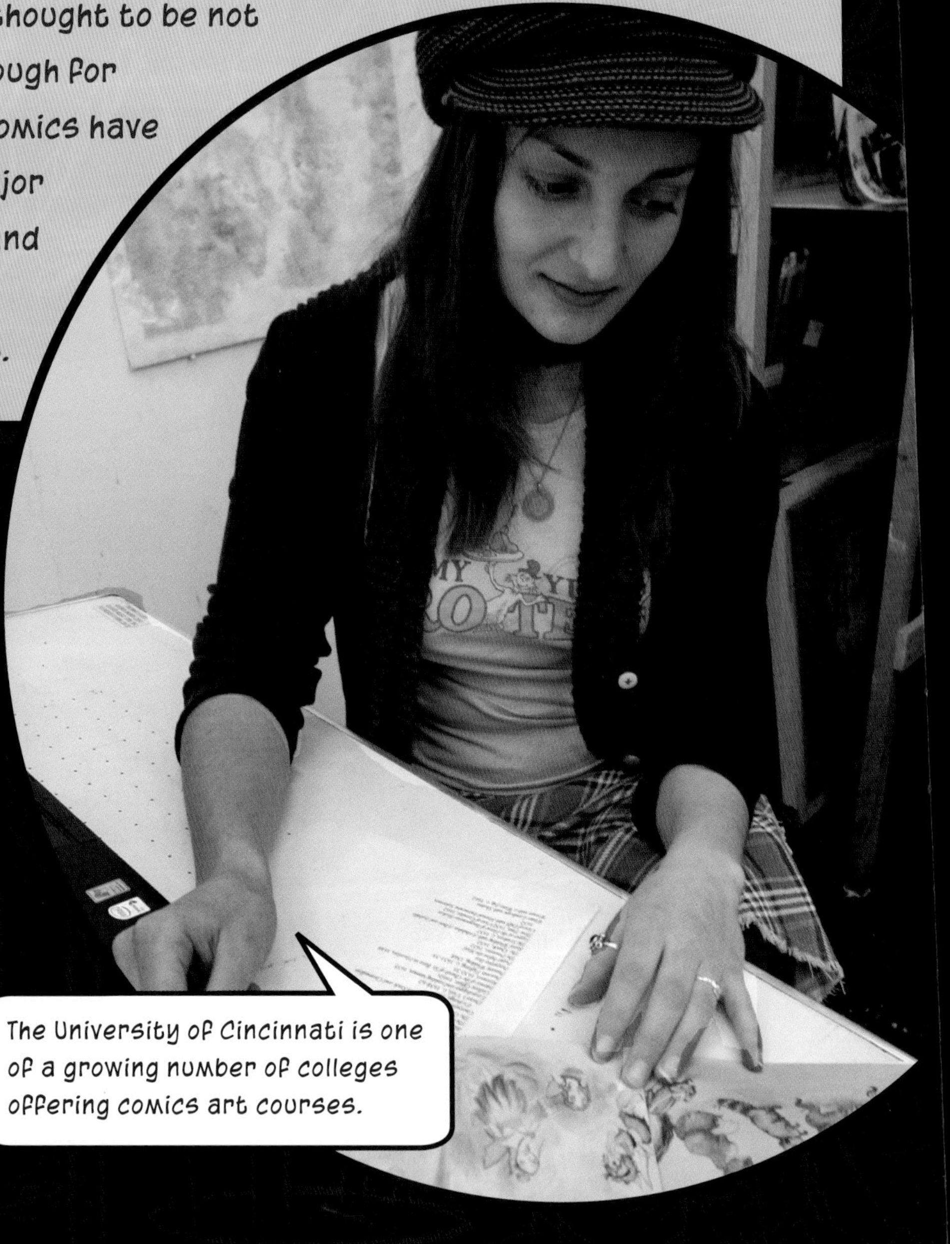

The University of Cincinnati is one of a growing number of colleges offering comics art courses.

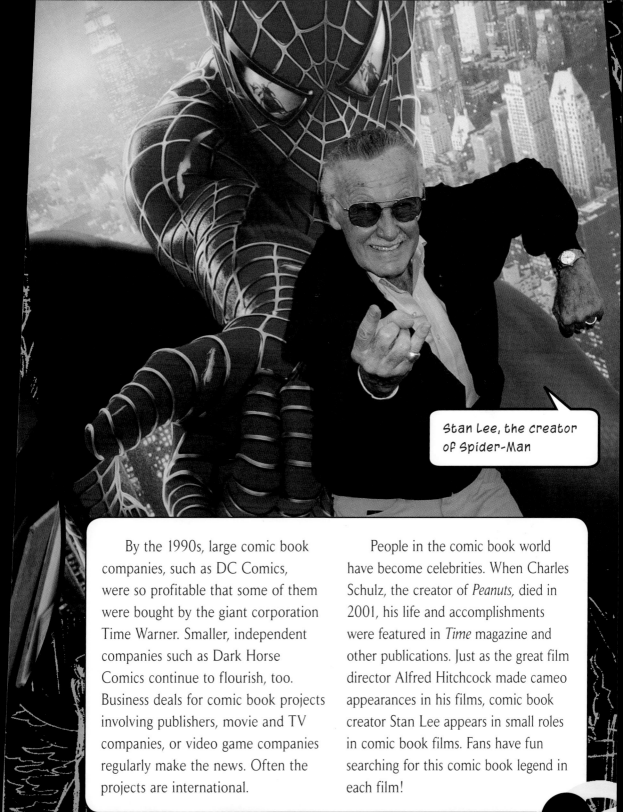

Stan Lee, the creator of Spider-Man

By the 1990s, large comic book companies, such as DC Comics, were so profitable that some of them were bought by the giant corporation Time Warner. Smaller, independent companies such as Dark Horse Comics continue to flourish, too. Business deals for comic book projects involving publishers, movie and TV companies, or video game companies regularly make the news. Often the projects are international.

People in the comic book world have become celebrities. When Charles Schulz, the creator of *Peanuts,* died in 2001, his life and accomplishments were featured in *Time* magazine and other publications. Just as the great film director Alfred Hitchcock made cameo appearances in his films, comic book creator Stan Lee appears in small roles in comic book films. Fans have fun searching for this comic book legend in each film!

Fans and Fandom

Fans now get together not just in small comic book stores but at large gatherings that themselves make the news. In 2009 more than 125,000 fans, comic book creators, and professionals in related fields attended the 40th annual Comic-Con meeting at San Diego's Convention Center. This yearly event previews new comics and comic-based products. Panels of people in front of large audiences discuss hot topics in the comic book world. The yearly Eisner Awards, the comic book equivalent of the Academy Awards, are also announced at Comic-Con.

At Comic-Con and other fan gatherings, some enthusiastic fans dress up as their favorite comic, manga, or anime characters. Their costumes—called cosplay—are an enjoyable part of fandom. Sometimes fans who know each other through the Internet meet in person at fan conferences. Meeting comic book celebrities at conferences is also a thrill.

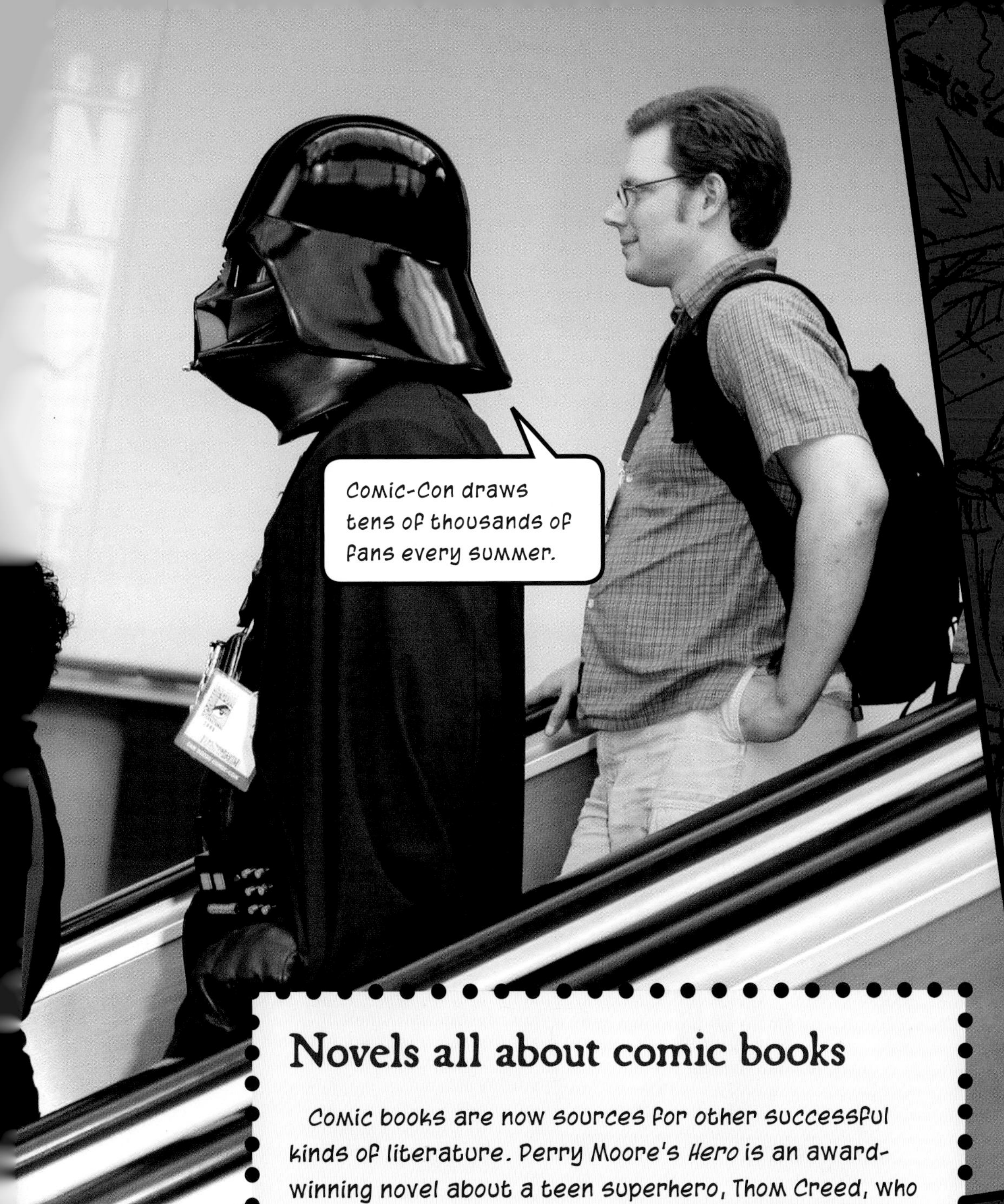

Comic-Con draws tens of thousands of fans every summer.

Novels all about comic books

Comic books are now sources for other successful kinds of literature. Perry Moore's *Hero* is an award-winning novel about a teen superhero, Thom Creed, who is gay. Austin Grossman's *Soon I Will Be Invincible* is a novel told partly by a supervillain, Dr. Impossible. It starts with his childhood. Tom De Haven's *It's Superman!* is a novel reimagining Clark Kent's life growing up in 1920s and 1930s America.

Cultural successes

Exhibits of comic book art have been displayed by major art museums, including the Louvre in Paris, France. There are museums entirely devoted to the history of comic books and comic book art in New York City, San Francisco, California, and Brussels, Belgium.

Graphic novels—competing against traditional books—have won major literary awards. In 1992 Art Spiegelman's family history, *Maus*, won a special Pulitzer Prize. In 2007 Gene Luan Yang's graphic novel *American Born Chinese* won the Printz Award for excellence in young adult literature. Graphic novels have also been used to explore and explain world religions. Osamu Tezuka created a series of graphic novels about the life of Buddha to communicate the values of Buddhism to readers both young and old.

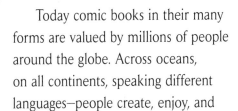Today comic books in their many forms are valued by millions of people around the globe. Across oceans, on all continents, speaking different languages—people create, enjoy, and learn from comic books. Think of that the next time you hold a graphic novel in your hand, visit a comics Web site, or watch an anime!

The National Gallery of Victoria in Melbourne, Australia, hosted an exhibition of Osamu Tezuka's work. "The Marvel of Manga" then moved to the Asian Art Museum in San Francisco.

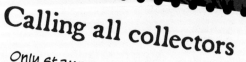

Calling all collectors

Only stamps and coins are collected more often than comics. Even the president of the United States collects comics. Some rare comic books are now worth big bucks. These are the most valuable issues:

* Action Comics #1 (June 1938), in which Superman debuted. One copy is now worth at least $440,000.

* Detective Comics #1 (May 1939), in which Batman first appeared. A copy is now worth at least $375,000.

Michael Chabon and comic books

Writer Michael Chabon loves comic books. His novel *The Amazing Adventures of Kavalier and Clay* follows the lives of two imaginary comic book creators. It won many awards, including the Pulitzer Prize for fiction in 2001. Chabon has since written stories for several new comic books—titled *The Escapist*—based on fictional comics created by characters in his novel.

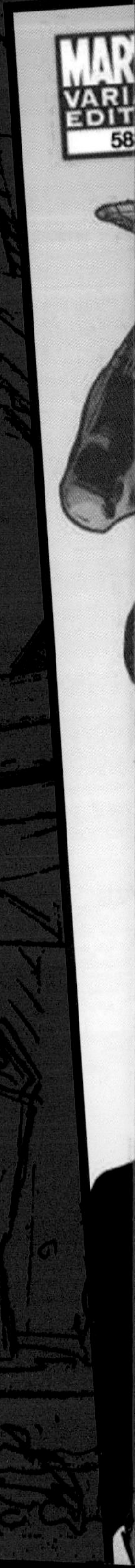

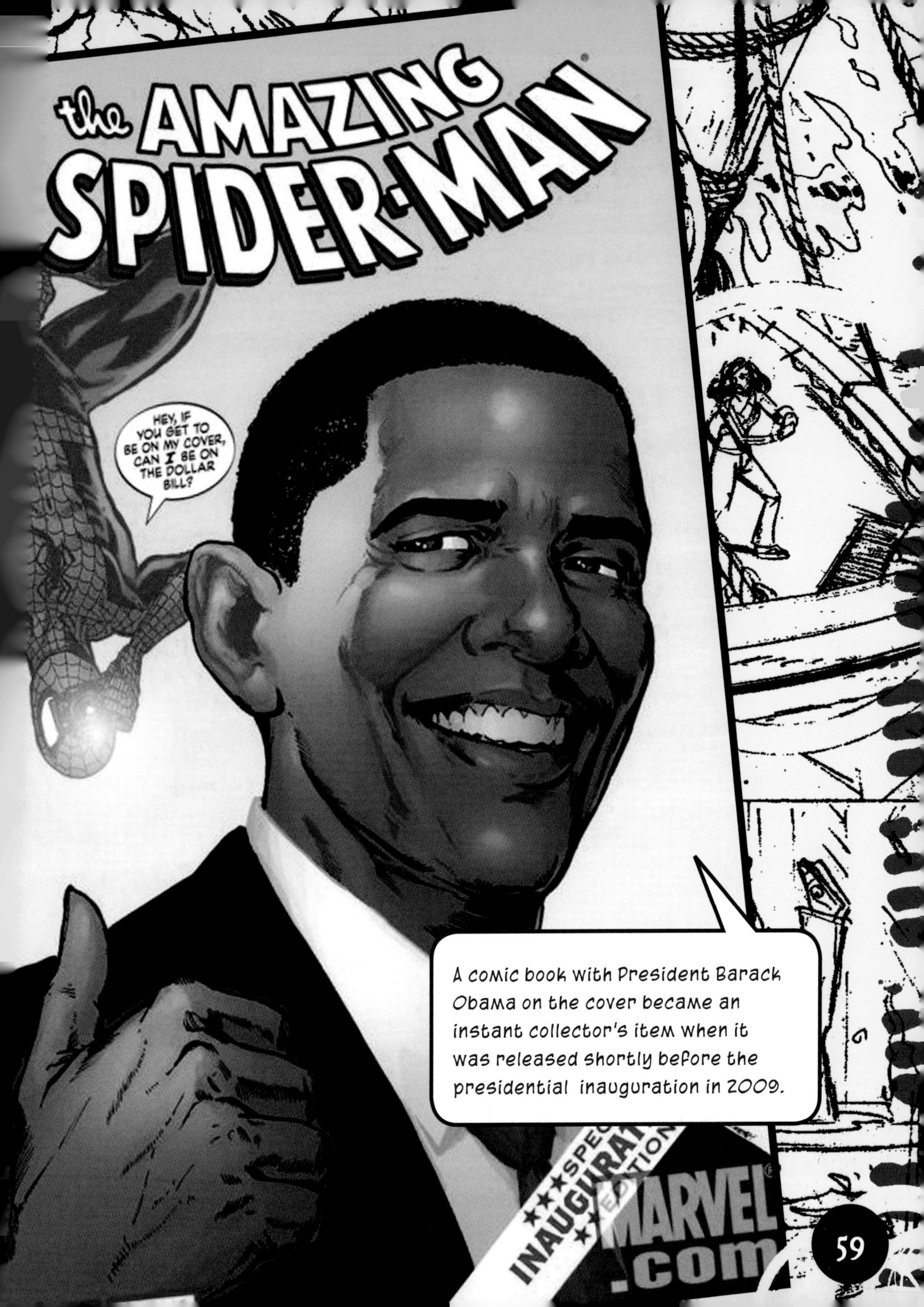
the AMAZING SPIDER-MAN
HEY, IF YOU GET TO BE ON MY COVER, CAN I BE ON THE DOLLAR BILL?
MARVEL .com

A comic book with President Barack Obama on the cover became an instant collector's item when it was released shortly before the presidential inauguration in 2009.

Comic Books

Timeline

1897 •••••••••••• First book of collected newspaper comic strips (*The Yellow Kid Magazine*) is published

1929 •••••••••••• First *Tintin* comic book is published in Europe

1933 •••••••••••• First comic book of previously published material (*Funnies on Parade*) is published in the U.S.

1935 •••••••••••• First comic book of all-new material, *New Fun #1*, is published.

1938 •••••••••••• First appearance of Superman in *Action Comics*

1951 •••••••••••• First *Astroboy* comic book is published in Japan; *Superman* television show debuts in the United States

1954 •••••••••••• Publication of *Seduction of the Innocent*; creation of Comics Code Authority that set standards for comic books

1962 •••••••••••• First *Spider-Man* comic book is published in the United States

1963 •••••••••••• First publication of *X-Men* comics

1969 •••••••••••• First African-American superhero in a mainstream U.S. comic book (*The Falcon*) appears

1978 •••••••••••• Publication of what is often considered the first graphic novel, *A Contract With God*

1992 •••••••••••• Graphic novel *Maus* wins a special Pulitzer Prize for literature

2007 •••••••••••• Graphic novel *American Born Chinese* wins the Printz Award for young adult literature

2008 •••••••••••• Picture book *The Wall: Growing Up Behind the Iron Curtain* wins the Silbert Award, given to the best information book for young people; Batman movie *The Dark Knight* sets box office records

2009 •••••••••••• Walt Disney Company agrees to buy Marvel for $4 billion

Glossary

anime	cartoons and cartoon movies made in Japan, often using characters and plots taken from written manga
ban	to forbid or make something illegal within a certain area
censor	to remove material considered morally or politically offensive or harmful
controversy	public disagreement or dispute between groups of people
cosplay	creating or wearing a comic book character costume at a comic book convention
discrimination	unfair treatment of a person or group, often because of race, religion, gender, sexual preference, or age
fan	someone enthusiastically interested in something, such as comics or movies
graphic novel	book-length fiction or nonfiction comic book that today is accepted as an art form
juvenile delinquent	young person who commits crimes; the term became popular in the 1950s
manga	comic books created in Japan and read worldwide; their style has influenced other comic book cultures
scanlations	downloads of comic books written in other languages that have been translated into English; their images are scanned
seduction	luring someone from good behavior to bad
sidekick	slang word for a close companion or helper, often used in detective novels or movies and superhero comics

Answers to quiz on page 41:

Triplicate Girl can split into three identical bodies.

Bouncing Boy can inflate like a ball and bounce.

Phantom Girl can pass through solid objects.

Ferro Lad is a mutant with the power to transform himself into living iron.

Cosmic Boy can generate magnetic fields.

Beast Boy has the ability to morph into any animal he chooses.

Additional Resources

Beatty, Scott. *The DC Comics Encyclopedia: The Definitive Guide to the Characters of the DC Universe.* New York: DK Publishing, 2008.

Beatty, Scott. *Wonder Woman: The Ultimate Guide to the Amazon Princess.* New York: DK Publishing, 2003.

Conroy, Mike. *500 Great Comic Book Action Heroes.* Hauppauge, N.Y.: Barron's, 2003.

Gravett, Paul. *Graphic Novels: Everything You Need to Know.* New York: HarperCollins Publishers, 2005.

Krensky, Stephen. *Comic Book Century: The History of American Comic Books.* Minneapolis: Twenty-first Century Books, 2008.

Misiroglu, Gina, ed. *The Superhero Book: The Ultimate Encyclopedia of Comic-Book Icons and Hollywood Heroes.* Detroit: Visible Ink Press, 2004.

Sanderson, Peter. *X-Men: The Ultimate Guide.* New York: DK Publishing, 2006.

Sís, Peter. *The Wall: Growing Up Behind the Iron Curtain.* New York: Farrar, Straus and Giroux, 2007.

Spiegelman, Art. *Maus: A Survivor's Tale.* New York: Pantheon Books, 1997.

Yang, Gene Luen. *American Born Chinese.* New York: First Second, 2006.

FactHound

FactHound offers a safe, fun way to find Internet sites related to this book. All of the sites on FactHound have been researched by our staff.

Here's all you do:
Visit *www.facthound.com*
FactHound will fetch the best sites for you!

Look for the other books in this series:

GAMERS UNITE!
The Video Game Revolution

PLAY IT LOUD!
The Rebellious History of Music

YOU CAN'T READ THIS!
Why Books Get Banned

Select Bibliography

Benton, Mike. *The Comic Book in America: An Illustrated History.* Dallas: Taylor Publishing, 1989.

Benton, Mike. *Superhero Comics: The Illustrated History.* Dallas: Taylor Publishing, 1991.

Dorfman, Ariel, and Armand Matellart. *How to Read Donald Duck: Imperialist Ideology in the Disney Comic.* London: International Editions, 1984.

Feiffer, Jules, ed. *The Great Comic Book Heroes.* New York: Dial, 1965.

Fingeroth, Danny. *Disguised as Clark Kent: Jews, Comics, and the Creation of the Superhero.* New York: Continuum, 2007.

Fingeroth, Danny. *Superman on the Couch: What Superheroes Really Tell Us About Ourselves and Our Society.* New York: Continuum, 2004.

Goulart, Ron. *Comic Book Culture: An Illustrated History.* Portland, Ore.: Collectors Press, 2007.

Gravett, Paul. *Manga: Sixty Years of Japanese Comics.* New York: Collins Design, 2004.

Hajdu, David. *The Ten-Cent Plague: The Great Comic-Book Scare and How It Changed America.* New York: Farrar, Straus and Giroux, 2008.

McCloud, Scott. *Understanding Comics: The Invisible Art.* Northampton, Mass.: Tundra Pub., 1993.

Pilcher, Tim, and Brad Brooks. *The Essential Guide to World Comics.* London: Collins and Brown, 2005.

Robbins, Trina. *A Century of Women Cartoonists.* Northampton, Mass.: Kitchen Sink Press, 1993.

Robbins, Trina. *The Great Women Superheroes.* Northampton, Mass.: Kitchen Sink Press, 1996.

Stromberg, Fredrik. *Black Images in the Comics: A Visual History.* Seattle: Fantagraphics Books, 2003.

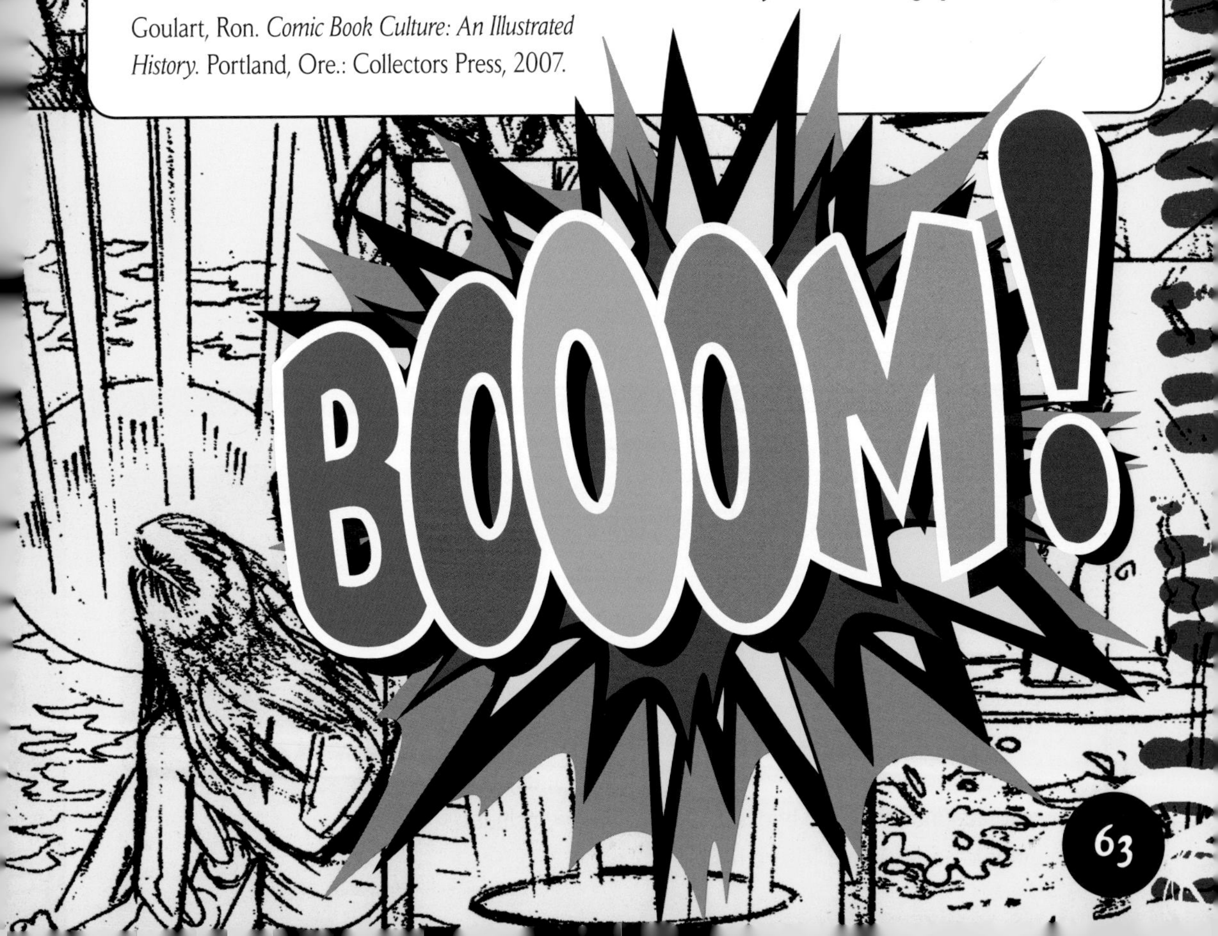

BOOOM!

Index

About the Author

Natalie M. Rosinsky is an award-winning author of more than 100 books, articles, and activities for young readers, including *Write Your Own Graphic Novel*. She earned graduate degrees in English from the University of Wisconsin-Madison and has worked as a high school teacher and college professor, as well as a corporate trainer. Natalie read all kinds of comic books as a kid and now includes graphic novels in her leisure reading.